Barry Lynn, an ordained minister in the United Church of Christ and an attorney, is executive director of Americans United for Separation of Church and State. He formerly served as legislative counsel for the American Civil Liberties Union in Washington, D.C.

Marc D. Stern is a graduate of Columbia Law School and is codirector of the Commission on Law and Action of the American Jewish Congress, where he specializes in the First Amendment's religion clauses.

Oliver S. Thomas is an ordained minister and currently serves as special counsel to the National Council of Churches of Christ in the U.S.A. He formerly taught church-state law at Georgetown University Law Center and served as general counsel to the Baptist Joint Committee.

S0-AFN-918

Also in this series

THE RIGHT TO RELIGIOUS LIBERTY

THE BASIC ACLU GUIDE TO RELIGIOUS RIGHTS

SECOND EDITION
Completely Revised and Updated

Barry Lynn
Marc D. Stern
Oliver S. Thomas

General Editor of the Handbook Series
Norman Dorsen, President, ACLU 1976–1991

SOUTHERN ILLINOIS UNIVERSITY PRESS
CARBONDALE AND EDWARDSVILLE

98 97 96 95   4 3 2 1

Library of Congress Cataloging-in-Publication Data

Lynn, Barry.
    The right to religious liberty : the basic ACLU guide to religious
rights / Barry Lynn, Marc D. Stern, Oliver S. Thomas. — 2d ed.,
completely rev. and updated.
        p.   cm. — (An American Civil Liberties Union handbook)
    1. Freedom of religion—United States. 2. United States—
Constitutional law—Amendments—1st. 3. Church and state—United
States. I. Stern, Marc D., 1950–   . II. Thomas, Oliver S., 1955– .
III. Title.   IV. Series.
KF4783.L96   1995
342.73′0852—dc20
[347.302852]   94-13635
ISBN 0-8093-1966-7   CIP
ISBN 0-8093-1967-5 (pbk.)

The paper used in this publication meets the minimum requirements of
American National Standard for Information Sciences—Permanence of
Paper for Printed Library Materials, ANSI Z39.48-1984. ∞

Contents

Preface

This guide sets forth your rights under present law and offers suggestions on how they can be protected. It is one of a continuing series of handbooks published in cooperation with the American Civil Liberties Union (ACLU).

Surrounding these publications is the hope that Americans, informed of their rights, will be encouraged to exercise them. Through their exercise, rights are given life. If they are rarely used, they may be forgotten and violations may become routine.

This guide offers no assurances that your rights will be respected. The laws may change, and in some of the subjects covered in these pages, they change quite rapidly. An effort has been made to note those parts of the law where movement is taking place, but it is not always possible to predict accurately when the law *will* change.

Even if laws remain the same, their interpretation by courts and administrative officials often varies. In a federal system such as ours there is a built-in problem since state and federal laws differ, not to speak of the variations among states. In addition, there is much diversity in the ways in which particular courts and administrative officials interpret the same law at any given moment.

If you encounter what you consider to be a specific abuse of your rights, you should seek legal assistance. There are a number of agencies that may help you, among them ACLU affiliate offices, but bear in mind that the ACLU is a limited-purpose organization. In many communities there are federally funded legal service offices that provide assistance to persons who cannot afford the costs of legal representation.

In general, the rights that the ACLU defends are freedom of inquiry and expression; due process of law; equal protection under the law; and privacy. The authors in this series have discussed other rights (even though they sometimes fall outside the ACLU's usual concern) in order to provide as much guidance as possible.

These books have been planned as guides for the people directly affected: thus the question-and-answer format. (In some areas there are more detailed works available for experts.) These guides seek to raise the major issues and inform the nonspecialist of the basic law on the subject. The authors of these books are themselves specialists who understand the need for information at "street level."

If you encounter a specific legal problem in an area discussed in one of these handbooks, show the book to your attorney. Of course, he or she will not be able to rely exclusively on the handbook to provide you with adequate representation. But if your attorney hasn't had a great deal of experience in the specific area, the handbook can provide helpful suggestions on how to proceed.

> Norman Dorsen, General Editor
> Stokes Professor of Law
> New York University School of Law

The principal purpose of this handbook, as well as others in this series, is to inform individuals of their legal rights. The authors from time to time suggest what the law should be, but their personal views are not necessarily those of the ACLU. For the ACLU's position on the issues discussed in this handbook, the reader should write to Public Education Department, ACLU, 132 West 43d Street, New York, NY 10036.

Acknowledgments

Each of us owes debts to a variety of persons, not all of whom can be mentioned. We would especially acknowledge our gratitude to Norman Dorsen, general editor of this series; our assistants, Regina Haden, Rosemary Bevard, Libby Ivins, and Denise Simmonds (who prepared the final manuscript); and, of course, our wives, Joanne Lynn, Lisa Thomas, and Marcy Stern.

We pray our children—Rachel and Sarah Thomas; Zahava, P'nina, Gedalia, Yair, and Chana Stern; and Christina and Nicholas Lynn—will take advantage of their constitutional liberties to pursue their respective religious traditions and will share the responsibility to preserve the gift of those freedoms for their children.

Introduction

The casual observer of the religious scene might regard it as more than a little strange that the American Civil Liberties Union should commission two ordained Christian ministers and an Orthodox Jewish rabbinical school dropout to prepare a book on religious liberty. Critics of the ACLU's position on church-state separation often accuse it of being godless and militantly atheistic. Why, then, should three religious lawyers prepare a book on religious liberty for the ACLU?

The facts, of course, are far more complicated. In the first place, the American Civil Liberties Union has diligently and vigorously advanced claims that the religious liberty of individual believers and religious institutions are infringed upon by government. More importantly, the three authors of this book believe, with the American Civil Liberties Union, that keeping religion and state separate is not godless but in the best interest of both religion and state.

The questions and answers in this book address a broad range of issues dealing with church-state separation and religious liberty. We have attempted to present the law as objectively as possible. We do not necessarily agree with each of the decisions we cite, nor would each one of the three of us resolve every case the same way. Still, we have attempted to give the interested reader a general sense of where the law stands. Each of us took primary responsibility for drafting different chapters of the book, but we each reviewed all of the book and thus bear full responsibility for all of it.

THE RIGHT TO
RELIGIOUS LIBERTY

I

The Establishment Clause

What is the purpose of the Establishment Clause?
The purpose of both the Establishment Clause and the Free
Exercise Clause is to guarantee religious liberty. The Establishment Clause seeks to accomplish this by prohibiting Congress
from passing laws "respecting an establishment of religion."
Note that the clause forbids more than an establishment of
religion. It forbids even laws *respecting* an establishment of
religion. Thus, a law that does not actually establish religion
yet involves or concerns an establishment of religion would
appear to violate the clause.[1]

**Does the Establishment Clause apply to other branches of
the federal government besides Congress?**
Yes, the Establishment Clause restricts the legislative, executive, and judicial branches of government.[2]

What about state and local governments?
They, too, are subject to the restriction against laws respecting an establishment of religion. The Due Process Clause of
the Fourteenth Amendment, which provides that no person
may be deprived of "life, *liberty* or property without due process of law," has been interpreted as applying the religion
clauses to state and local governments.[3]

What is meant by "an establishment of religion"?
There is much debate over the meaning of "an establishment
of religion." Some argue that an establishment of religion refers
only to the designation of a single state church.[4] Thus, aid to
religion generally would not be prohibited by the Establishment Clause as long as no religion received preferential treatment.[5] Under this view, government could favor religion over
irreligion but not one particular denomination over another.
The more likely meaning, however, is that an establishment
of religion refers to the endorsement of either a single religion
or religion generally. According to this point of view, govern-

ment should be neutral in matters of religion, preferring neither one religion over another nor religion over irreligion.[6]

Those who espouse this stricter separation of church and state point out that multiple establishments of religion (whereby nondiscriminatory aid could flow to a number of different churches or sects) were commonplace in the thirteen colonies. Some colonies provided for the establishment of the Christian religion in general, while others were more discriminatory, supporting only Protestant churches. In fact, when the First Amendment was drafted, no single-church establishment of religion existed in the United States. Multiple establishments were the rule. Even James Madison's famous *Memorial and Remonstrance Against Religious Assessments* was written in response to a bill providing for the support of teachers of the Christian religion in general.

Obviously, the framers were aware that in eighteenth-century America "an establishment of religion" included multiple establishments, and any analysis of their intent in drafting the First Amendment must recognize this awareness.

When presented with an amendment allowing the very sort of multiple establishments suggested by nonseparationists, Congress rejected it out of hand. Indeed, the Senate thrice rejected amendments that would have prohibited the establishment of one religious sect in preference to others while providing for aid to religion in general. Both houses ultimately agreed upon the much broader prohibition contained in the First Amendment.[7]

The Supreme Court in the 1947 decision *Everson v. Board of Education* adopted the separationist point of view[8] and, in one of the most famous passages in constitutional law, Justice Hugo Black wrote:

> The "establishment of religion" clause of the First Amendment means at least this: Neither a state nor the Federal Government can set up a church. Neither can pass laws which aid one religion, aid all religions, or prefer one religion over another. Neither can force nor influence a person to go to or to remain away from church against his will or force him to profess a belief or disbelief in any religion. No person can be punished for entertaining or professing religious beliefs or disbeliefs, for church atten-

dance or non-attendance. No tax in any amount, large or small, can be levied to support any religious activities or institutions, whatever they may be called, or whatever form they may adopt to teach or practice religion. Neither a state nor the Federal Government can, openly or secretly, participate in the affairs of any religious organizations or groups and vice versa. In the words of Jefferson, the clause against establishment of religion by law was intended to erect "a wall of separation between Church and State."[9]

Has the Court adopted a particular legal test to assist in deciding cases arising under the Establishment Clause?

Yes. In the 1971 case, *Lemon v. Kurtzman*,[10] the Court adopted a three-part test, derived from its earlier cases, to assist it in deciding cases under the Establishment Clause. In order for government action to be permissible under the Establishment Clause, it must (1) have a secular purpose, (2) have a primary effect that neither advances nor inhibits religion and (3) not cause excessive governmental entanglement with religion.

The fact that a law may have a religious purpose or be motivated by religion[11] does not mean it is unconstitutional as long as it also has a bona fide secular or civic purpose (*e.g.*, housing the homeless). Similarly, a law that has a remote or incidental effect of advancing religion is not unconstitutional as long as the effect is not a "primary" effect (*e.g.*, providing fire and police protection to churches and synagogues). The effect prong can be violated, however, in a number of different ways, including government action that creates a symbolic union of church and state[12] or that delegates discretionary governmental power to a religious body.[13]

Finally, some entanglement between church and state is permissible. Excessive entanglement is not. When determining whether entanglement is excessive, courts will consider the nature of (1) the aid provided, (2) the institution receiving the aid, and (3) the resulting relationship between that institution and the government. Excessive entanglement is most likely to occur when government attempts to monitor or involve itself in the affairs of pervasively sectarian institutions such as churches, synagogues, other places of worship, and primary and secondary parochial schools.[14] For example, in *Aguilar v. Felton* the Supreme Court struck down a remedial education program offered in parochial schools that required state employees to monitor the program to ensure that no funds were being used to promote religion.[15]

In recent years, the *Lemon* test has been modified by the addition of Justice O'Connor's endorsement test. This test asks whether, in the eyes of an "objective" observer, the particular government action has the purpose or effect of endorsing religion.[16] The endorsement test is designed to prevent any citizen from feeling like a political outsider because of his or her religious affiliation or lack of it. The endorsement test is sometimes collapsed into the effects prong (part two) of *Lemon's* three-part test.[17] Both tests prohibit significant government promotion or sponsorship of religion or support or aid to it.

Is compulsion of religious practice or belief a necessary element to an Establishment Clause violation?

No. The Supreme Court has held repeatedly that compulsion is not a necessary element to an Establishment Clause violation.[18] Recent Supreme Court opinions suggest, however, that the Court may be moving toward making compulsion or coercion an element of its Establishment Clause analysis.[19] Professor Douglas Laycock has pointed out that a test based on coercion would be an insufficient protection for religious liberty.[20] Even noncoercive sponsorship, support, and endorsement of religion may violate the conscience of minority faiths and nonbelievers. One's standing in the political community should not be affected by the existence or intensity of one's religious commitments.

NOTES

1. *See* Laycock, *"Nonpreferential" Aid to Religion: A False Claim about Original Intent*, 27 Wm. & Mary L. Rev. 875 (1986); L. Levy, *The Establishment Clause: Religion and the First Amendment* (1986).
2. *North Carolina Civil Liberties Union v. Constangy*, 947 F.2d 1145 (4th Cir. 1991); *Lamont v. Woods*, 948 F.2d 825 (2d Cir. 1991).
3. *Cantwell v. Connecticut*, 310 U.S. 296 (1940); *Everson v. Board of Education*, 330 U.S. 1 (1947).
4. *E.g.*, R. Cord, *Separation of Church and State: Historical Fact and Current Fiction* (1982).
5. *Wallace v. Jaffree*, 472 U.S. 38, 91 (1985) (Rehnquist, J., dissenting).

6. *E.g.*, *Torcaso v. Watkins*, 367 U.S. 488, 495 (1961); *Everson v. Board of Education*, 330 U.S. 1 (1947) (see text accompanying note 9 *infra*; *Wallace v. Jaffree*, 472 U.S. 38, 52–54 (1985).

7. T. Curry, *The First Freedoms: Church and State in America to the Passage of the First Amendment* (1986); W. Miller, *The First Liberty: Religion and the American Republic* (1985); L. Levy, *The Establishment Clause: Religion and the First Amendment* (1986).

8. While the Court split 5 to 4 over the constitutionality of providing bus service to students in parochial schools, all nine justices agreed that the Establishment Clause mandates neutrality not only among religions but between religion and irreligion.

9. 330 U.S. 1, 15–16.

10. 403 U.S. 602 (1971).

11. *Clayton v. Purdy*, 884 F.2d 376 (8th Cir. 1989).

12. *School District of the City of Grand Rapids v. Ball*, 473 U.S. 373, 389–91 (1985).

13. *Larken v. Grendel's Den*, 459 U.S. 116, 123–25 (1982).

14. *Lemon v. Kurtzman*, 403 U.S. 602 (1971); *Tilton v. Richardson*, 403 U.S. 672 (1971).

15. 473 U.S. 402 (1985). Under the entanglement prong of *Lemon*, the Court has from time to time expressed concern over a challenged action's potential for political divisiveness along religious lines. *E.g.*, *Lemon v. Kurtzman*, 403 U.S. 602, 622–25 (1971); *Meek v. Pittenger*, 421 U.S. 349, 359–62 (1975). More recently, the question of political divisiveness has been confined to cases involving direct financial subsidies to religious institutions such as parochial schools. *Mueller v. Allen*, 463 U.S. 388, 403 (1983).

16. *Lynch v. Donnelly*, 465 U.S. 668, 687, 691–92 (1984) (O'Connor, J., concurring):

> The Establishment Clause prohibits government from making adherence to a religion relevant in any way to a person's standing in the political community. Government can run afoul of that prohibition in two principal ways. . . . The second and more direct infringement is government endorsement or disapproval of religion. Endorsement sends a message to nonadherents that they are outsiders, not full members of the political community, and an accompanying message to adherents that they are insiders, favored members of the political community.
>
> The proper inquiry under the purpose prong of *Lemon*, I submit, is whether the government intends to convey a message of endorsement or disapproval of religion.
>
> Focusing on the evil of government endorsement or disap-

proval of religion makes clear that the effect prong of the *Lemon* test is properly interpreted not to require invalidation of a government practice merely because it in fact causes, even as a primary effect, advancement or inhibition of religion. . . . What is crucial is that a government practice not have the effect of communicating a message of government endorsement or disapproval of religion.

17. *See, e.g., County of Allegheny v. American Civil Liberties Union,* 492 U.S. 573 (1989).

18. *E.g., Committee for Public Education and Religious Liberty v. Nyquist,* 413 U.S. 756, 768 (1973).

19. *County of Allegheny v. American Civil Liberties Union,* 492 U.S. 573, 659 (1989) (Kennedy, J., concurring in part and dissenting in part): "Our cases disclose two limiting principles: government may not coerce anyone to support or participate in any religion or its exercise; and it may not, in the guise of avoiding hostility or callous indifference, give direct benefits to religion in such a degree that it in fact "establishes a [state] religion or religious faith, or tends to do so" (citations omitted). *See also Lee v. Weisman,* 505 U.S. ____, 112 S. Ct. 2649, 2678 (1992) (Scalia, J., dissenting).

20. Laycock, *supra* note 1.

II

Religion and Public Education

Special rules about the place of religion and government apply to the nation's public schools. The Supreme Court has insisted that the public schools not promote or denigrate religion, religious or antireligious values as such, or sponsor official religious ceremonies.[1] There are hundreds of federal and state court decisions on the subject, only some of which are discussed here. The basic outlines of the law are now well understood, although there are several areas where the courts have not yet agreed on an answer.

In general, the cases may be divided into four categories: (1) school-sponsored religious activities; (2) preferential access to pubic schools by religious organizations for purposes of proselytizing or spreading the faith; (3) religion in the curriculum; and (4) the rights of students or teachers to freedom of expression and freedom of religious practice within the public schools. Again speaking generally, the first three categories were decided first, with cases in the last category being decided more recently.

With the exception of the aid to parochial school cases (*see* chapter 3), no area of church-state law has been as controversial, nor been in controversy for as long, as questions about the place of religion in the public schools.

The earliest public schools were founded by Protestant churches, for whom reading was a necessary religious skill because church members had to be able to read the Bible for themselves. In these early public schools, religion was an important part of the school program. There were daily prayers acceptable to most Protestant denominations as well as readings from the Protestant King James Bible.

In the 1830s, large numbers of Catholic immigrants came to the United States. These immigrants' religious beliefs and practices were very different from those of Protestants, and they saw the public schools as extensions of the Protestant churches. Bitter conflicts over religion in the schools followed, leading to riots, expulsion of Catholics from some public schools, prosecution of parents for encouraging the truancy of their children (because the children would not read the King James Bible), the burning of convents, and even deaths.

The immigrants, through their churches, sought two remedies for the unfairness they saw in the public school system: (1) equal funding for Catholic parochial schools and (2) the elimination of the most obvious Protestant practices from the public schools. The first demand was everywhere rejected, although it is still being pressed. The demand for elimination of obviously sectarian practices gradually met with greater success. By the late nineteenth century or early twentieth century, a few state courts had either banned religious exercises from the public schools as inconsistent with state constitutions or insisted that students be given some choice about what form their religious observances would take (*e.g.*, the freedom to choose the Bible from which they would read). Still, where schools did not change, most courts upheld widely accepted school religious practices such as prayer or Bible reading, typically on the theory that these helped to develop good character and morals in students. Gradually most schools came to accept the notion that religious practices could not be forced on unwilling students. They allowed religious practices to continue, but excused those who did not want to participate.[2]

By the 1950s, the growing religious diversity of America and a split between modernist (so-called mainline Protestant) and nonmodernist (evangelical or fundamentalist) Protestants, together with a growing number of nonbelievers, shifted the battle once again. More and more, it was recognized that there was no common religious ritual, or at least, that the Protestant religious forms traditionally used in the public schools were too sectarian to be used when there were so many children from Catholic, Jewish, Hindu, Moslem, or atheistic homes. The public schools responded in two ways. One was to attempt to write bland, nonsectarian prayers ("God is great, God is good, and we thank him for our food").[3] The other response was for the public schools to renounce responsibility for religious education but to help churches and synagogues offer religious instruction to children who wanted it.

In 1947 the Supreme Court held for the first time that the Establishment Clause of the First Amendment applied to the public schools.[4] Thus, the Constitution limited the role the public schools could play in helping churches provide children with religious education. Later, in the 1960s, the Court banned almost all forms of in-school religious ceremonies and instruction.[5] Religious advocacy in the curriculum was also held inconsistent with the Establishment Clause. Contrary to popular belief, however, the Court never outlawed teaching about religion or all references to God or the Bible.[6] Regrettably, some schools, teachers, and textbook writers thought that the Court had done so and eliminated most references to religion from the public schools.

The court decisions requiring the pubic schools to avoid religious practice were not implemented all at once. Those districts that were religiously homogeneous often managed to avoid change. Changes in the classroom came only with demographic change in the community. When a substantial number of people of different religions moved into a school district, districts were forced to respond.

Resentment at the forced abandonment of traditional religious practices, together with a broad popular belief that the courts and schools had gone too far in eliminating religion from the public schools, led to a backlash in the 1980s. In part, this backlash was exploited by politicians looking for a symbolic issue to fuel popular concern over the ills of American society. But, it would be a mistake to dismiss the entire reaction as if it were merely a political ploy. There was a broad feeling that the courts had erred and that they had in fact been enlisted in an antireligious crusade.

At first, this reaction took the form of a direct assault on the principle that the schools could not encourage religious practices on a voluntary basis. (By the 1980s almost no one argued for obligatory religious practices in the public schools.) When these efforts proved unsuccessful, those who wanted greater religious activity in the public schools switched to emphasizing the rights of individual students or teachers to engage in religious practices or to speak on religious subjects within the public schools. Advocates of religion in the school thus adopted two of the tactics of traditional civil libertarians. They emphasized individual rights (*e.g.*, freedom of speech) and equality between religion and nonreligion, the very arguments earlier made by opponents of religion in the schools.

These efforts have raised some hard questions about the exact line between not allowing schools to sponsor or assist religious activity and recognizing the rights of individual students and teachers to speak of their religious beliefs or observe their religion in the public schools.

For all the criticism from both sides, it ought to be said that on the whole the courts have succeeded in striking a balance that is respectful of all the values at issue.

What is the general rule about religion in the public schools?

The general rule is that the public schools may not advocate or discourage religion, engage in religious ceremonies, such as prayers or invocations, urge religious or antireligious points of view on students, or consciously shape the curriculum to avoid subjects or points of view that are at odds with the teachings of religion.[7]

Does this mean that the public schools cannot mention God or religion at all?

Not at all, although some people mistakenly believe that the Supreme Court has banned all mention of religion in the public schools. Religion is an important part of human life and is an important element of most societies. History, literature, art, and music cannot be taught accurately and completely without teaching about religion. The history of religion itself is an important subject in the history of ideas. Instruction *about* religion is perfectly acceptable under the Constitution, as long as the school's approach is academic rather than devotional.[8]

What is the source of these rules?

The Establishment Clause of the First Amendment to the Constitution, which prohibits laws respecting an establishment of religion, has been the most important source of law in this area. Most states have similar constitutional provisions prohibiting the public schools from teaching sectarian doctrine. (Some states, however, have constitutions that mention the state's interest in teaching religion.)[9] On the other hand, the Free Exercise Clause and the Free Speech Clause of the First Amendment to the Constitution set limits on how far schools may go in regulating or prohibiting student religious activity.[10]

Do the prohibitions of the Establishment Clause apply to students themselves?

Not as a general matter. The Constitution applies only to

the activity of the government, not private parties. Students are thus free to read their Bibles, recite the rosary, or pray before meals or math tests.[11] Public school officials are prohibited by the Constitution from interfering with these activities. For the same reason, private schools are not bound by these strictures. However, when student activity extends beyond the individual, participation must be truly voluntary. Courts take into account that students are present at school because of compulsory attendance laws. Generally, students may not engage in religious activities that are disruptive or infringe upon the rights of others.

May schools begin the school day or school activities with prayer?

No. When a school begins the day with a prayer it signals to its students that they should pray. The schools may not do that, anymore than they may discourage students from praying. It does not matter whether the prayer is composed or selected by the school board, or composed or selected by a teacher or a student volunteer.

Does it matter that students are not compelled to participate in the prayer?

Again the answer is no. The Constitution prohibits the state from advocating religion, whether or not anyone is forced to participate.[12] A majority of justices have recognized that a student in a classroom or other school setting has relatively little choice but to accede to school officials if they are to avoid the ridicule of classmates.[13] Moreover, some students are afraid to say no to anything a teacher suggests even if it is presented as voluntary. Thus, even if school officials label a religious activity "voluntary," it may not be in practice.

Are school-sponsored prayers prohibited in all school activities?

Yes. The courts have applied the no-school-sponsorship-of-prayer rule to graduation ceremonies, school assemblies, and athletic events, as well as to daily prayers in the classroom.[14] A few courts in relatively older cases have held that public schools may sponsor baccalaureate services where prayers are recited and sermons preached.[15] These cases are probably incorrect in light of a recent Supreme Court decision barring prayers at graduation,[16] although the lower courts are divided over whether a school district may permit students to determine on their own whether to pray. Sounder decisions rule that they may not.[17] Of course, churches are free to sponsor baccalaureate services with religious content and to invite all the students at a particular public school. School officials should make clear that such a ceremony is not sponsored or endorsed by the school.[18]

May the Bible be read or taught in the public schools?

It depends. The Bible may not be read as part of a ceremonial opening exercise or used as a book of moral or spiritual instruction. On the other hand, the Bible is one of the formative books of Western society and has shaped its history, politics, ideas, literature, art, and music. Religion may be studied in an objective manner so that students may have knowledge of this influential book and appreciate its impact on the world and culture. Thus, Bible-as-literature courses are constitutional provided that they are not taught from a religious point of view.[19] School libraries may include the Bible and other important religious works, but no particular faith's literature should be favored over others.[20]

Can a teacher claim a right to pray with his or her students or to teach religious values?

No. Although a teacher has some rights of freedom of expression in the classroom, he or she is an agent of the state while teaching and may not take advantage of that position to press personal religious views on students. Generally, a teacher may not pray or read the Bible in the classroom either with, or in the presence of, students; nor may a teacher advocate sectarian points of view such as the doctrine that God created the world. Similarly, teachers should not denigrate or inquire into the religious points of view of students.[21] Schools may discharge teachers who ignore these restrictions.

May a school display religious passages such as the Ten Commandments on the walls of the classroom?

Not unless it is a temporary display that has a distinct educational purpose. Any passage of the Bible may be studied in an objective manner; however, the purpose of a wall display generally is not to teach about the displayed passage but to encourage students to venerate the passage or to sponsor an attitude of religious veneration.[22]

May a school announce a moment of silence at the beginning of the school day?

Probably, if it does not encourage students to use the moment of silence to pray. If all the school does is tell students they may use the time as they see fit, the activity does not violate the Constitution.[23] However, students may not be told to assume a position commonly associated with prayer, such as bowing the head.[24]

Are not these restrictions unfair to those whose religion demands that prayer accompany daily activities?

No. Nondisruptive individual prayer is permissible in the public school. Thus, it is possible for those who want to pray quietly before each of life's activities to do so. It is even possible for groups of like-minded students to engage in communal prayer before or after school under certain limited circumstances.[25] Asking schools to endorse such activities or imposing them on students who do not wish to participate simply cannot be accommodated within our constitutional system. Schools may explain to students that the fact that there are no school-sponsored prayers is not an expression of disapproval of prayer. It is rather an expression of respect for the rights of believers and nonbelievers alike.

May public schools cooperate with churches and synagogues to provide religious classes?

Yes. These arrangements are called *released-time classes.* In such arrangements, students are released early to attend religious classes. They are permissible only off campus. School officials may not encourage participation. Religious schools bear the burden and expense of soliciting participants. School officials must also arrange a suitable and fair alternative for those students who choose not to participate in released-time programs.[26] Schools are under no constitutional obligation to operate a released-time program.

Can nonstudent religious groups enter school grounds to either teach classes or otherwise speak to students under school auspices?

Generally, no. Certainly adult religious groups cannot teach religious classes during the school day or read Bible stories during lunch hour. [27] Neither can members of the clergy or other persons with a religious message address student assemblies or be allowed to meet with students during the school day. The common practice of allowing youth ministers preferential entry into the public schools is undoubtedly unconstitutional. An exception to this rule might exist if a school allowed all community groups access to students (even if only at a set time and place), in which case there are indications that some courts would require equal access for religious groups. However, it is probable that because of the Establishment Clause, special restrictions on religious access are appropriate because the state is by force of compulsory education laws providing an involuntary audience. [28] Only limited involvement of outside adults is permissible under the Equal Access Act.

May a school district exclude all teaching about the theory of evolution?

No. The Supreme Court has held that schools may not tailor their curricula to avoid offending religious groups. The theory of evolution—that is, that species of life have evolved over time in a natural way—is accepted in broad detail by the overwhelming weight of scientific thought. Although some religious believers insist that this theory is contradicted by the Bible, the state may not suppress a recognized body of knowledge to avoid offending religious believers. [29]

May a biology teacher tell students that the theory of evolution conclusively repudiates a literal reading of the Bible?

Again, the answer is no. Just as the public schools may not act to further religion, neither may they set out purposefully to attack specific religious beliefs. [30]

Can a school offer "equal time" to religious and scientific theories of human origins?

No. Several years ago Louisiana passed a law calling for equal treatment of the generally accepted theories of evolution and a doctrine espoused by certain religious groups called *scientific creationism*. The Supreme Court found that this law was enacted to promote a religious doctrine and therefore was unconstitutional. The Court did state that a variety of scientific theories, including those critical of evolution, could be taught in the classroom. Schools may teach *about* religious theories of origins. They may not be endorsed or taught as truth.[31]

Is it unconstitutional for a school to teach values?

Not at all. There are many values that are generally accepted in our society, such as honesty, diligence, respect for the rights of others, respect for law, and the like. Teaching these values and others present no constitutional difficulty. Indeed, any values may be taught as long as there is some civic or nonsectarian justification.

Some people in my community object that if schools teach secular values they are teaching secular humanism, a world view they regard as hostile to religion. Do they have a legitimate complaint?

Almost certainly not. *Secular humanism* is a phrase with two distinct meanings, and it is important to be precise about them. There is an ideology called "Secular Humanism" that is partially explained in a document called the *Humanist Manifesto*.[32] Among other things, the *Manifesto* denies that humans may properly rely on any supernatural authority to determine their ethical choices. That doctrine, and those closely associated with it, may not be taught in the public schools. However, we are aware of no case where this has been done.

Critics of the public schools also use the term to mean the failure of schools to advocate religious teachings or the use of textbooks that promote values unacceptable to a particular faith. Courts have made clear that the failure to teach religious values does not violate the Constitution. On the contrary, schools are required to be neutral in matters of faith. Similarly, the fact that civic values taught in schools coincide with the teachings of a particular religion, whether Christian or humanist, does not mean that schools are guilty of promoting that religion. Most religions teach honesty, but this does not mean public schools are forbidden from teaching honesty.[33] While schools generally cannot choose textbooks based on religious objections, a textbook could be rejected if it ignored the role of religion in a particular subject (*e.g.*, history) or treated religion unfairly.[34]

May schools excuse students from reading selections that they find religiously offensive?

Schools may, and frequently do, excuse students from readings they find religiously offensive. However, most courts have held that schools need not do so, even if they can do so without difficulty. This is because courts have held that mere exposure to ideas with which a student disagrees is not a substantial burden on the free exercise of religion. Whether or not schools agree to excuse students on religious grounds, they may not suppress the offending texts altogether, so that no other student may use them. On the other hand, students may not be compelled to accept as true a proposition with which they disagree on religious grounds.[35]

May a student be compelled to recite the Pledge of Allegiance?

No. However, the Pledge is not objectionable simply because it contains a reference to God.[36] The courts generally reason that the routine use of the phrase "under God" has deprived it of religious significance.

How may public schools observe Christmas and other religious holidays?

Schools may not *celebrate* religious holidays as religious holidays. However, schools may teach about the meaning of these holidays, and the schools may include music and holiday displays as long as these are done for a legitimate educational purpose and have a generally secular (*i.e.*, nonsectarian) effect.[37]

Some years ago, a group of leading religious and educational groups agreed upon a set of guidelines (known as the *joint statement*) to help schools deal with this problem. These guidelines are repeated below in slightly shortened form in the following eight questions and answers.

Do religious holidays belong in the curriculum?

The study of religious holidays may be included in elementary and secondary curricula as opportunities for teaching about religions. Such study serves the academic goals of educating students about history and cultures, as well as the traditions of particular religions within pluralistic society.

When should teaching about religious holidays take place?
On the elementary level, natural opportunities arise for discussion of religious holidays while studying different cultures and communities. In the secondary curriculum, students of world history or literature have opportunities to consider the holy days of religious traditions.

How should religious holidays be treated in the classroom?
Teachers must be alert to the distinction between teaching about religious holidays, which is permissible, and celebrating religious holidays, which is not. Recognition of and information about holidays may focus on how and when they are celebrated, their origins, histories and generally agreed-upon meanings. If the approach is objective and sensitive, neither promoting nor inhibiting religion, this study can foster understanding and mutual respect for differences in belief.

Teachers will want to avoid asking students to explain their beliefs and customs. An offer to do so should be treated with courtesy and accepted or rejected depending upon the educational relevancy.

Teachers may not use the study of religious holidays as an opportunity to proselytize or to inject personal religious beliefs into the discussions. Teachers can avoid this by teaching through attribution, *i.e.*, by reporting that "some Buddhists believe . . ."

May religious symbols be used in public school classes?
The use of religious symbols, provided they are used only as examples of cultural and religious heritage, is permissible as a teaching aid or resource. Religious symbols may be displayed only on a temporary basis as part of the academic program. Students may choose to create artwork with religious symbols. Teachers should not encourage or discourage such creations.

May religious music be used in public schools?
Sacred music may be sung or played as part of the academic study of music. School concerts that present a variety of selec-

tions may include religious music. Concerts should avoid programs dominated by religious music, especially when these coincide with a particular religious holiday.

The use of art, drama, or literature with religious themes also is permissible if it serves a sound educational goal in the curriculum but not if used as a vehicle for promoting religious belief.

What about Christmas?

Decisions about what to do in December should begin with the understanding that public schools may not sponsor religious devotions or celebrations; study about religious holidays does not extend to religious worship or practice.

Does this mean that all seasonal activities must be banned from the schools? Probably not, and in any event such an effort would be unrealistic. The resolution would seem to lie in devising holiday programs that serve an educational purpose for all students—programs that make no students feel excluded or identified with a religion not their own.

Holiday concerts in December may appropriately include music related to Christmas and Hanukkah, but religious music should not dominate. Any dramatic productions should emphasize the cultural aspects of the holidays. Nativity pageants or plays portraying the Hanukkah miracle are not appropriate in the public school setting.

In short, while recognizing the holiday season, none of the school activities in December should have the purpose, or effect, of promoting or inhibiting religion.

What about religious objections to some holidays?

Students from certain religious traditions may ask to be excused from classroom discussions or activities related to particular holidays. Some holidays considered by many people to be secular (for example, Halloween and Valentine's Day) are viewed by others as having religious overtones.

Excusal requests may be especially common in the elementary grades, where holidays often are marked by parties and similar nonacademic activities. Such requests are routinely granted.

In addition, some parents and students may make requests for excusals from discussions of certain holidays even when treated from an academic perspective. If focused on a limited, specific discussion, such requests may be granted in order to strike a balance between the student's religious freedom and the school's interest in providing a well-rounded education.

Administrators and teachers should understand that a policy or practice of excusing students from a specific activity or discussion cannot be used as a rationale for school sponsorship of religious celebrations or worship for the remaining students.

May students be absent for religious holidays?

Sensitive school policy on absences will take account of the religious needs and requirements of students. Students should be allowed a reasonable number of excused absences, without penalties, to observe religious holidays within their traditions. Students may be asked to complete makeup assignments or examinations in conjunction with such absences.[38]

Must schools excuse students from attendance on their religious holidays?

Until the Supreme Court decision in *Employment Division v. Smith*, (*see* chapter 7), it was generally assumed that schools could not compel students to attend on their religious holidays nor penalize them for not doing so (*e.g.*, refusing to provide a makeup examination). The Court once remarked that schools that excuse such students are acting in accordance with the best of American traditions.[39] *Smith* cast the duty to accommodate students' religious needs into doubt. Still, the duty may have survived *Smith* because the observance of holidays is not only a religious obligation but an example of the rights of parents to control the upbringing of their children. Excusal for religious holidays may thus be the sort of hybrid right that the Court indicated in *Smith* would be subject still to compelling interest analysis. Generally, schools have no compelling reason for not accommodating their students' holiday observances. In many states, the right to miss school on religious holidays without penalty is guaranteed by statute, usually by way of exception to the compulsory education laws. The Religious Freedom Restoration Act (chapter 16) restores the law to its pre-*Smith* state.

In any event, schools may certainly excuse students without

violating the Establishment Clause.[40] Of course, any policy of excusal must be applied equally to students of all faiths.[41]

May the public schools close on religious holidays?
Yes, if they do so for nonreligious reasons. The schools may close because many students or teachers will not attend.

If a group such as the Gideons wishes to distribute Bibles to students who express an interest in receiving them, may the school cooperate in this project?
The school may not have teachers hand out Bibles,[42] permit the Gideons or a similar group into its classrooms or otherwise facilitate the distribution of religious literature by outside groups. On the other hand, a public school may not ban the Gideons or anyone else from distributing religious literature on the public sidewalk in front of public schools.[43]

Can students speak of their religious views in the classroom?
Yes and no. A classroom is a place for the exchange of ideas, and religious ideas may not be excluded. Thus, students may write and speak on religious themes and draw pictures with religious themes. However, students in a classroom are a captive audience, and the teacher may need to intervene to protect students from a sermon offered by a classmate.[44]

Can students distribute religious literature to fellow students?
Yes, subject to certain restrictions. The federal courts have repeatedly held that students have the right under the Free Speech Clause of the First Amendment to distribute literature to their fellow students provided it will not cause a breakdown of order or impinge on the rights of fellow students.

In general, students may distribute religious literature to fellow students. School officials cannot ban literature just because it is religious. However, they may impose reasonable "time, place, or manner" restrictions directing when, where, and how *all* student literature is distributed. Schools must provide reasonable alternative ways for the material to be distributed. Thus, school officials may specify certain times for distribution of material (*e.g.*, lunch hour, before and after school, or during class breaks), the place where it may take place (*e.g.*, not in hallways, locker rooms, or places where the activity is not easily supervised), and the way in which it is distributed (*i.e.*, from fixed locations rather than roving distribution).

It is likely that school officials may insist on predistribution screening to guard against the distribution of obscene, defamatory, or disruptive materials. Such a policy should provide for a speedy decision, a statement of reasons for rejection, and a prompt appeal process. In classrooms themselves, school officials have greater leeway and can probably ban the distribution of religious literature. One court has held that schools may exclude all nonstudent prepared literature.[45]

Are there limits to what students may distribute?

Yes. If the literature threatens to disrupt the school or infringe on the rights of others, distribution may be banned.[46] This standard is flexible, and depends on all the circumstances. What is permissible in a senior high school may not be permissible in the third grade. For example, a flyer warning that those who do not accept Christ will burn in hell forever could probably be excluded from an elementary school but not necessarily from a senior high school.

May schools impose restrictions on student religious speech?

Our nation's commitment to free speech ordinarily "requir[es] people to put up with annoyance at uninvited speech,"[47] at least until the speaker is asked to stop. Thus, in the ordinary case, government may not ban speech in order to protect ordinary citizens from the "annoyance" of putting up with offensive speech.

The courts recognize, however, that in places where people are present by force of law—where the listeners are a captive audience—a different rule may apply. Schoolchildren are not present in school voluntarily and thus might be thought to constitute a captive audience.

There is as yet no clear rule in the courts. It would seem that outside the classroom, students have at least one opportunity to proselytize a fellow student in a nondisruptive manner, but when asked by the student to stop, they must do so. School officials are free to intervene if the student proselytizers attempt to harass, coerce, or isolate those who are not receptive to their message. In the classroom, where students are not free to walk away, teachers may exert greater control, but not to the point of excluding every statement of religious belief.[48]

Perhaps no firm rule can be stated other than to say that school officials should try to protect both the rights of those who wish to speak on religious matters as well as the rights of students who do not wish to be compelled to listen to a sermon.

May students gather together for student-initiated religious meetings during noninstructional time?

Yes, if schools allow any other student group not directly related to the school's curriculum to meet, it must allow students to meet and discuss religion. For many years, the courts debated whether student religion clubs had a constitutional right to meet. Before a definite ruling could be obtained, Congress passed the Equal Access Act,[49] which guaranteed student religious clubs the same rights as enjoyed by other student clubs not related to the school curriculum.[50]

Does the Act apply to all public schools?

The Act applies to all public secondary schools that receive federal funds.[51] Whether a school is a secondary school is determined by state law.[52]

Are there restrictions on what schools may do under the Equal Access Act?

Yes. Schools may not sponsor a noncurriculum-related club.[53] School officials may not control the clubs nor encourage participation in noncurriculum clubs;[54] nor may they permit outsiders to control or regularly attend club meetings.[55] A school may insist that some member of the school staff attend all meetings, but only for purposes of keeping order.[56] However, schools cannot force staff to attend meetings where the speech is contrary to the beliefs of the staff member.[57] Only clubs that are student initiated are protected under the Act.

What may a school do if a club is disorderly?

The Act authorizes school officials to maintain order and protect the "well-being" of students and teachers and to ensure that attendance is voluntary.[58] Also, school officials need not permit meetings that are "otherwise unlawful"—*e.g.*, a meeting to plan the assassination of the principal. Mere advocacy of illegal conduct or the legalization of presently outlawed activity cannot be grounds for banning a club. In other words, a club that seeks to lower the drinking age cannot be banned.

The Act does not directly address the question of whether a school may ban hate groups or clubs that discriminate on the grounds of religion.[39] No court has yet addressed these difficult questions.

May schools impose a minimum or maximum number of members in noncurriculum clubs?

No.[60]

Is the Act constitutional?

Yes. In *Board of Education v. Mergens*,[61] the Supreme Court upheld the constitutionality of the Equal Access Act. The Court reasoned that since religious clubs were only one of many clubs that would be meeting, students could not conclude that the school was favoring religion by permitting religious clubs. Moreover, the Court noted that clubs met before or after school, and that students had to affirmatively choose to participate. The Court also noted that schools were free to inform students that the school did not endorse the agenda of any club (or specifically religious clubs). Finally, the Court noted that high school students were mature enough to understand the difference between clubs the school sponsored and clubs it supported.

Must schools permit noncurriculum clubs to meet?

No. A public school may decide to ban *all* noncurriculum clubs. However, once a school decides to permit even one noncurriculum club to meet, it must permit all such clubs.[62]

What is a noncurriculum club? Is the term defined by statute?

The Act does not define what is meant by a noncurriculum club. The Supreme Court has offered the following definition (496 U.S. at ___):

[W]e think that the term "non-curriculum related student group" is best interpreted broadly to mean any student group that does not directly relate to the body of courses offered by the school. In our view, a student group directly relates to a school's curriculum if the subject matter of the group is actually taught, or will soon be taught, in a regularly offered course; if the subject matter of the group concerns the body of courses as a whole; if participation in the group is required for a particular course; or if participation in the group results in academic credit. We think this limited definition of groups that directly relate to the curriculum is a common sense interpretation of the Act that is consistent with Congress' intent to provide a low threshold for triggering the Act's requirements.

For example, a French club would directly relate to the curriculum if a school taught French in a regularly offered course or planned to teach the subject in the near future. A school's student government would generally relate directly to the curriculum to the extent that it addresses concerns, solicits opinions, and formulates proposals pertaining to the body of courses offered by the school. If participation in a school's band or orchestra were required for the band or orchestra classes, or resulted in academic credit, then those groups would also directly relate to the curriculum. The existence of such groups at a school would not trigger the Act's obligations.

Can students be compelled to wear dress they consider immodest?

Probably not, although it is less clear whether students can avoid gym classes because others are dressed immodestly. Although federal law generally prohibits sex-segregated classes, the Department of Education has ruled that students with religious objection to mixed physical education classes may be offered separate classes.[63]

May a school district insist on teaching sex education courses even if they conflict with parental values or a student's religion?

Probably, although it is rare for a school sex education program to be mandatory. Schools generally do not insist on students attending these classes over parental objection, and some state statutes provide for mandatory excusal. With the AIDS crisis, some school districts have begun to insist on attendance. Courts are likely to uphold a decision to require attendance in sex education courses based upon the state's overriding interest in protecting the health and safety of students. The courts have also held that mandatory sex education courses do not infringe on the right of parents to control the education and moral upbringing of their children. [64]

Is it permissible for schools to insist that children be vaccinated over religious objections?

Yes, because vaccination protects the health and safety of children and of others. [65] However, because public health would generally not be seriously affected if the few students who object on religious grounds were exempted, many states have excused persons with religious objection from the vaccination requirement. Some of these limitations have been declared unconstitutional because they extend only to adherents of "recognized churches," a limitation inconsistent with the Constitution's protection of individual believers who are not members of a recognized church. [66]

Can a school district prohibit teachers from wearing religious garb to class?

Yes, but it is not required to do so. About one hundred years ago, many states passed laws banning teachers from wearing religious garb to class. There was a twofold motivation of the statutes: to keep religion and state separate and to exclude members of the Catholic clergy, especially nuns, from the public schools. Although some courts have held these statutes unconstitutional, more recent decisions uphold the constitutionality of these statutes and also reject challenges to them based on civil rights laws requiring accommodation of religious practice. [67] However, it is generally understood that these statutes do not apply to the display of religious jewelry or temporary religious markings, such as wearing ashes on Ash Wednesday. [68]

Must a school district accommodate the holiday observance of its teachers?

Yes. Title VII of the 1964 Civil Rights Act requires that all employers, including the public schools, make reasonable efforts to accommodate the religious practices of employees.

However, they need not incur undue hardship to do so. If a request for accommodation would require the expenditure of more than a *de minimis* amount of money or violate the seniority provisions of a collective bargaining agreement, it need not be granted.[69]

The choice of accommodation lies solely in the hands of the employer. So long as the accommodation is reasonable, the employee may not object that some other alternative exists that is less onerous for the employee and no more burdensome for the employer. Thus, leave without pay will almost always satisfy the duty to accommodate.[70]

The duty to accommodate extends beyond the problem of holiday observance. It extends to a religiously based refusal to teach courses, *e.g.*, a refusal to teach a course on biology including large sections of evolutionary theory.[71]

NOTES

1. Whenever we refer to "religious" in this chapter, the reader should understand that these constitutional doctrines under discussion also ban school sponsorship of antireligious ceremonies or encouragement of an antireligious attitude on the part of teachers or students. Because "antireligious" cases have only rarely arisen, the text only refers to a preference for religion.
2. For a history of church-state developments in the public schools, see L. Pfeffer, *Church State and Freedom* (1967) and D. Ravitch, *The Great School Wars* (1974).
3. See, *e.g.*, *DeSpain v. DeKalb County Community School District 428*, 384 F.2d 836 (7th Cir. 1967).
4. *Illinois ex rel. McCollum v. Bd. of Education*, 333 U.S. 203 (1948) (invalidating in-school released-time program). *Cf. Everson v. Bd. of Education*, 330 U.S. 1 (1947) (holding Establishment Clause binds state and local government but upholding constitutionality of transporting pupils to parochial schools).
5. *School District of Abington Twshp. v. Schempp*, 374 U.S. 203 (1963) (Lord's Prayer); *Engel v. Vitale*, 370 U.S. 421 (1962) (state-composed opening prayer).
6. *Epperson v. Arkansas*, 393 U.S. 97 (1967); *School District of Abington Twshp. v. Schempp*, *supra*, 374 U.S. at 225.
7. *Lee v. Weisman*, 505 U.S. ____ (1992); *Wallace v. Jaffree*, 472 U.S. 38 (1985); *Epperson v. Arkansas*, 393 U.S. 97 (1967); *School District*

of Abington Twshp. v. Schempp, 374 U.S. 203 (1963); *Engel v. Vitale*, 370 U.S. 421 (1962).

8. *School District of Abington Twshp. v. Schempp, supra.*

9. For a somewhat dated, but still largely accurate, summary, see C. J. Antieau, P. M. Carroll & T. Burke, *Religion Under the State Constitutions* (1965).

10. *See* below at notes 44–71.

11. Maryland *Op. of the Att'y. Gen.* No. 84-031; *Kansas Op. of the Att'y Gen.* 88-12.

12. *Allegheny County v. Greater Pittsburgh ACLU*, 492 U.S. 573 (1989); *School District of Abington Twshp. v. Schempp, supra*, 374 U.S. at 224, n. 9.

13. *Lee v. Weisman*, 505 U.S. at ____ (1992).

14. *Collins v. Chandler Unified School Dist.*, 644 F.2d 759 (9th Cir. 1981) (school assemblies); *Jager v. Douglas County School Dist.*, 862 F.2d 824 (11th Cir. 1989) (football games); *Doe v. Aldine I.S.D.*, 563 F. Supp. 883 (S.D. Tex. 1982) (athletic events, pep rallies, and the like).

15. *See, e.g., Goodwin v. Cross Country School Dist.*, 394 F. Supp. 417 (E.D. Ark. 1973).

16. *Lee v. Weisman, supra*, 505 U.S. at ____.

17. *Compare Jones v. Clear Creek I.S.D.*, 977 F.2d 963 (5th Cir. 1992) with *Gearon v. Loudon County*, 849 F. Supp. 1092 (E. D. Va. 1993).

18. *Randall v. Pagan*, 765 F. Supp. 793 (W.D. NY 1991); *Verbena Methodist Church v. Chilton Bd. of Education*, 765 F. Supp. 704 (N.D. Ala. 1991).

19. *School District of Abington Twshp. v. Schempp*, 374 U.S. 201 (1963); *Grove v. Mead School District*, 753 F.2d 1528 (9th Cir. 1985); *Florey v. Sioux Falls School District*, 619 F.2d 1321 (8th Cir. 1980); *Todd v. Rochester Community Schools*, 41 Mich. App. 320, 200 N.W.2d 90 (1972); *Hall v. Bd. of School Commissioners*, 656 F.2d 999 (5th Cir. 1981) (invalidating sectarian bible-as-literature course).

20. *Roberts v. Madigan*, 921 F.2d 1047 (10th Cir. 1989).

21. *Webster v. New Lenox School District*, 917 F.2d 1009 (7th Cir. 1990); *Roberts v. Madigan*, 921 F.2d 1047 (10th Cir. 1991); *Breen v. Reinkel*, 614 F.Supp. 355 (W.D. Mich. 1985); *Rhodes v. Laurel Highlands School District*, 118 Pa. Cmwlth. 119, 544 A.2d 562 (1988); *Fink v. Board of* , 65 Pa. Cmwlth. 320, 442 A.2d 837 (1982), *app. dismissed for want of a substantial federal question*, 460 U.S. 1048 (1983); *LaRocca v. Board of Education*, 63 A.D.2d 1019, 406 N.Y.S.2d 348 (2d Dept.), *app. dismissed*, 46 N.Y.2d 770 (1978); *Alaska O.A.G.* File No. 663-88-0573 (Sept. 15, 1988); *Lynch v. Indiana State University*, 177 Ind. App. 176, 378 N.E.2d 900 (1978) (college professor may not pray with students); *Bishop v. Aronov*, 926 F.2d 1066 (11th Cir. 1991)

(teacher may not express even occasional religious views in college class). Similarly, a teacher may not insist on teaching creationism or resist teaching evolution. *Peloza v. Capistrano Unified School District*, 725 F.Supp. 1412 (C.D. Cal. 1992). A school board that knowingly acquiesces in a public-school teacher's practice of praying in the presence of students may be held liable for the actions of the teacher. *Steele v. Van Buren Public School District*, 845 F.2d 1492 (8th Cir. 1988).

22. *Stone v. Graham*, 449 U.S. 39 (1980).

23. *Wallace v. Jaffree*, 472 U.S. 38 (1985).

24. *Walter v. West Virginia Bd. of Education*, 610 F. Supp. 1169 (S.D. W.Va. 1985).

25. *See* the discussion below of the *Equal Access Act* at notes 49–60.

26. *Zorach v. Clauson*, 343 U.S. 306 (1952); *McCaulden v. Board of Education*, 333 U.S. 203 (1948); *Smith v. Smith*, 523 F.2d 121 (4th Cir. 1975).

27. *Doe v. Human*, 725 F. Supp. 1499 (W.D. Ark. 1989), *aff'd without opinion* 923 F.2d at 857 (8th Cir. 1980).

28. *Berger v. Rennselaer School District*, 982 F.2d 1160 (7th Cir. 1992) (distribution of Gideon Bibles).

29. *Epperson v. Arkansas*, 393 U.S. 97 (1967) (ban on teaching evolution).

30. *McCarthey v. Fletcher*, 207 Cal. App. 3d 130, 254 Cal. Rptr. 714 (1989).

31. *Edwards v. Aguillard*, 482 U.S. 578 (1987).

32. *Torcaso v. Watkins*, 367 U.S. 488, 495, n. 11 (1961).

33. *School District of Abington Twshp. v. Schempp*, 374 U.S. 203, 225 (1963); *Grove v. Mead School District*, 753 F.2d 1528, 1535–43 (9th Cir. 1985) (Canby, J., concurring); *Smith v. Board of Commissioners*, 827 F.2d 684 (11th Cir. 1987) (rejecting charge that books established secular humanism); *Brown v. Woodland Joint Unified School District*, 1992 W.L. 361696 (C.D. Cal. 1992), *app. pending*, (9th Cir. 1993); *Fleishfresser v. Directors School District*, 805 F. Supp. 584 (N.D. Ill. 1992), *aff'd*, _____ F.2d _____ (7th Cir. 1994) (both rejecting challenges to a textbook series on grounds that it promoted secular humanism).

34. *McCarthy v. Fletcher*, 207 Cal. App. 3d 130, 254 Cal. Rptr. 714 (1989).

35. *Compare Mozert v. Hawkins County Board of Education*, 827 F.2d 1058 (6th Cir. 1987); *Ware v. Valley Stream High School*, 75 N.Y.2d 114, 550 N.E.2d 420 (1989) (both stating general rule; *Ware*, however, carved out an exception on the facts before it) with *Davis* v. *Page*, 385 F. Supp. 395 (D. N.H. 1975); *Moody v. Cronin*, 484 F. Supp. 270 (C.D. Ill. 1979) (both holding excusal required if practicable).

Cf. Grove v. Mead School District, 753 F.2d 1528 ((9th Cir. 1983) (same, in *dicta*).

36. *Sherman v. Community Consolidated District*, 980 F.2d 437 (7th Cir. 1992).

37. *Florey v. Sioux Falls Independent School District*, 619 F.2d 1311 (8th Cir. 1980). Most of what follows flows from the holding in *Florey*.

38. *Church of God v. Amarillo Independent School District*, 670 F.2d 46 (5th Cir. 1982). *Cf. Zorach v. Clauson*, 343 U.S. 306, 313–14 (1952).

39. *Zorach v. Clauson*, 343 U.S. 306, 313–14 (1952); *Church of God v. Amarillo Independent School District*, 670 F.2d 46 (5th Cir. 1982). The right does not extend to rescheduling graduation. *Smith v. North Babylon School Dist.*, 844 F.2d 90 (2d Cir. 1988).

40. *Employment Division v. Smith*, 494 U.S. 872 (1990). Congress has enacted the Religious Freedom Restoration Act, mandating application of the prior rule of compelling interest. *See* chapter 16.

41. Oklahoma *Op. Att'y. Gen.* 87-11 (invalidating law applicable only to excusals for Jewish holiday observance).

42. *Berger v. Rennselaer School District*, 982 F.2d 1160 (7th Cir. 1993); *Gideons International v. Tudor*, 14 N.J. 31,100 A.2d 857 (1953); 65 Maryland *Op. Att'y. Gen.*, 186 (1980) (collecting cases and attorneys general opinion).

43. *Bacon v. Bradley-Bourbonnais High School District*, 707 F. Supp. 1005 (C.D. Ill. 1989).

44. *DeNooyer v. Livonia Public Schools*, 799 F. Supp 744 (E.D. Mich. 1992).

45. *Thompson v. Waynesboro Area School District*, 673 F. Supp. 1379 (M.D. Pa. 1987); *Clark v. Dallas I.S.D.*, 806 F. Supp. 116 (N.D. Tex. 1992); *Slotterback v. Interboro School District*, 721 F.2d 1189 (D. Col. 1989); *Nelson v. Moline School District*, 725 F. Supp. 965 (C.D. Ill. 1989); *Hedges v. Wauconda Community School District # 118*, 9 F.3d 3 (7th Cir. 1993).

46. *Tinker v. Des Moines School District*, 393 U.S. 503 (1969); *Gregoire v. Centennial School District*, 907 F. 1366 (3d Cir. 1991); *Clark v. Dallas I.S.D.*, 806 F. Supp. 116 (N.D. Tex. 1992).

47. *ISKCON v. Lee*, 112 S. Ct. 2701, 2719 (1992) (Kennedy, J., concurring).

48. *DeNooyer v. Livonia Public Schools*, 799 F. Supp. 744 (E.D. Mich. 1992).

49. A coalition of leading educational and religious groups also agreed on guidelines for implementing the Equal Access Act. Those guidelines are printed in appendix B.

50. 20 U.S.C. §§ 4071–74. For further details on the Act, see appendix B.
51. 20 U.S.C. § 4071(a).
52. 20 U.S.C. § 4072(1).
53. 20 U.S.C. § 4071(c)(2).
54. 20 U.S.C. § 4071(c)(1) and (2). *See Sease v. School Dist.*, 811 F. Supp. 783 (E.D. Pa. 1992), *app. pending.*
55. 20 U.S.C. § 4071(c)(5).
56. 20 U.S.C. § 4071(c)(3).
57. 20 U.S.C. § 4071(d)(4).
58. 20 U.S.C. § 4071(f).
59. An interesting, but as yet unanswered, question is whether a club that excludes other students on the basis of religion or race (or sex) acts "otherwise illegally" and thus can be banned. On one hand, these clubs meet in public schools where the state has a compelling interest in encouraging students of different backgrounds to interact with one another. On the other hand (particularly in religious meetings), there is generally a constitutional right not to associate with others. Many clubs have been willing to open their doors to all.
60. 20 U.S.C. § 4071(d)(6).
61. 496 U.S. 226 (1990).
62. *Id.*
63. *Moody v. Cronin*, 484 F. Supp. 270 (C.D. Ill. 1979).
64. *Ware v. Valley Stream High School*, 75 N.Y.2d 114, 551, N.Y. Supp. 2d 167, 550 N.E.2d 420 (1989) (mandating sexual education); *Arnold v. Board of Education*, 754 F. Supp. 853 (S.D. Ala. 1990) (mere discussion of abortion with student over parental objection not unconstitutional). Some scholars argue that schools cannot constitutionally withhold from students information that they may need in the future. Others criticize the existing rule as insufficiently protective of religion.
65. *Prince v. Commonwealth*, 321 U.S. 158 (1944); *Cude v. State*, 237 Ark. 927, 377 S.W.2d 816 (1964).
66. *Davis v. Maryland*, 294 Md. 370, 451 A.2d 107 (1982); *Brown v. Stone*, 378 So. 2d 219 (Miss. 1980) (both invalidating restrictions, and requiring all children to be vaccinated; *Davis* was overruled by statute that extended a privilege against inoculation to all persons with religious objections). The following cases invalidated a recognized church limitation on an exemption from vaccination and extended the exemption to members of nonrecognized churches: *Lewis v. Sobol*, 710 F. Supp. 506 (S.D.N.Y. 1989); *Avard v. Dupuir*, 376 F. Supp. 470 (D. N.H. 1974).
67. *U.S. v. Board of Education*, 911 F.2d 882 (3d Cir. 1990); *Cooper v. Eugene School District*, 301 Or. 358, 723 P.2d 298 (1986), *app.*

dismissed, 480 U.S. 942 (1987) (all upholding statute); *Gerhardt v. Heids*, 66 N.D. 444, 266 N.W.2d 718 (1936) (invalidating statute).

68. *EEOC v. Reads, Inc.*, 759 F. Supp. 1150 (E.D. Pa. 1991).

69. 42 U.S.C. §§ 2000e(i), *et seq.*; *TWA v. Hardison*, 432 U.S. 63 (1977); 2000e(j).

70. *Ansonia Board of Education v. Philbrook*, 479 U.S. 60 (1986).

71. South Dakota *Op. Att'y. Gen.* 89-19.

III

Aid To Religious Organizations

General

Can governments provide general safety and welfare services to religious institutions?

There is no question that governments may treat religious institutions as other groups for purposes of providing basic services like police and fire protection.

Only in extraordinary circumstances where a government is giving a special treatment to a religious institution will a First Amendment violation occur. For example, a city-owned electric utility was found to be acting unconstitutionally where it provided a special electricity subsidy to a Mormon Temple.[1] The court noted: "The electric subsidy given by the City impermissibly subsidized a religious institution. The City gave no other church such a subsidy. It conveyed a message of City support for the Latter-Day Saint faith."

Can government funds be used to defray costs of religious organizations' work?

The Supreme Court has tried to distinguish between religious organizations that are "pervasively sectarian" (for example, churches, theological seminaries, and elementary and secondary religious schools) and those that are merely "affiliated" with religious bodies. Ever since the late 1800s, courts have been reluctant to forbid government from funding the charitable or social service functions of religious groups. In 1899 the Supreme Court upheld such aid to a hospital operated by an order of Catholic nuns.[2] The Court recognized that the hospital was open to persons of all religious backgrounds and that it operated otherwise consistently with its charter to provide health services.[3]

The only other Supreme Court case on this matter was not decided until ninety years later. In *Bowen v. Kendrick*, a 5-to-4 majority ruled that it was not unconstitutional to provide federal funds for services relating to adolescent sexuality and pregnancy in religiously affiliated institutions. A determination would need to be made on a case-by-case basis whether any grantee was so "pervasively sectarian" that funds would be used to advance its religious mission.[4] In other words, the mere fact that congressional interest in sexual education or pregnancy counseling might coincide with the religious tenets of some grantees was not inherently unconstitutional. (Here, the statute specifically prohibited grants to institutions that "advocate, promote, or encourage" abortion.)

The four dissenters in *Kendrick* seemed to agree that government could pay religious institutions to provide many types of social services without constitutional difficulty. This program, however, included services that were educational in nature. The dissent noted that "[T]here is a very real and important difference between running a soup kitchen or a hospital, and counseling pregnant teenagers on how to make the difficult decisions facing them."[5]

On the other hand, courts have rejected the idea that government *must* include religious organizations in programs that pay private organizations to provide social services.[6]

In addition, subsidies to such institutions may permit actions that would not be permitted in secular facilities. For example, many courts have upheld the constitutionality of a provision of the Hill-Burton Act that permits religiously affiliated hospitals to refuse to perform abortion or sterilization procedures that violate their religious beliefs.[7]

In a number of recent pieces of federal legislation, federal aid to religious groups has been conditioned on such factors as the nondiscriminatory availability of the services to persons of any religion (aid to the homeless) and has forbidden the use of funds for building improvements (child care programs). Questions raised by some of these provisions have not been litigated, but on the basis of *Kendrick*, discussed above, it seems likely that only under specific fact situations where religious indoctrination could be demonstrated to be occurring with federal funds would the programs be deemed unconstitutional.

Aid to Religious Schools

Can governments provide financial assistance to religious schools?

Generally, no, but there are many exceptions to the rule that will be discussed below. These include some forms of aid given directly to students and aid to religiously affiliated colleges and universities that are not "pervasively sectarian."

Can public funds be used to transport children to religious schools?

Yes. In a 5-to-4 decision of the Supreme Court in 1947, the Court approved the payment of bus fares for students to go back and forth between their homes and the religious schools they were attending.[8] It concluded that such a program does no more than provide a general program to help parents transport their children (regardless of their religion) safely and expeditiously to and from accredited schools.[9] The Court likened it to providing police and fire protection to religious institutions as well as other types of community organizations. Although the majority acknowledged that there was a "possibility that some of the children would not be sent to the church schools if the parents were compelled to pay their children's bus fares out of their own pockets,"[10] it did not accept the minority's conclusion that this aid to secure religious teaching was an unconstitutional subsidy to the religious schools. Subsequently, it seems clear that bus transportation for parochial students may be funded even beyond school district lines, as long as public and private students are eligible on the same terms and the relative costs are roughly proportional.[11]

Can tax dollars be expended to buy textbooks that will be loaned to students in sectarian schools?

Yes, if the textbooks are purely secular and approved by public school authorities. A majority of the Supreme Court justified such loan programs, such as bus transportation to and from school, on the basis of the "child benefit theory." This approach assumes that the government is simply making available to all children the benefits of a general program of free schoolbooks.[12] The Court concluded there was no evidence that "supports the proposition that all textbooks, whether they deal with mathematics, physics, foreign languages, history, or literature, are used by the parochial school to teach religion." The dissenting justices believed that even in the selection of specific "secular" books, religious school authorities would inevitably make choices based on their religious views about these matters. In addition, some justices complained that money saved on such items as textbooks and transportation could be spent to further the schools' religious mission.[13]

May states subsidize the teaching of secular subjects in religious schools?

The Supreme Court has rejected several state schemes for achieving this result. Pennsylvania had attempted to reimburse teacher salaries for secular instruction in certain subjects. Rhode Island had tried a 15 percent salary supplement to teachers in private elementary schools if they taught only secular courses.[14] The Court found that primary and secondary parochial schools are "an integral part of the religious mission" of the parent religious body and "pervasively sectarian." Without any need to demonstrate bad faith, the Court found the potential for funding religious education too high: "In terms of potential for involving some aspect of faith or morals in secular subjects, a textbook's content is ascertainable, but a teacher's handling of a subject is not. We cannot ignore the danger that a teacher under religious control and discipline poses to the separation of the religious from the purely secular aspects of pre-college education. The conflict of functions inheres in the situation." Moreover, the "excessive and enduring entanglement" necessary to scrutinize the teachers' actions and the accounting procedure needed to determine secular and religious costs would also render these approaches unconstitutional as "direct aid" to religious schools.

What kinds of instructional materials and other supportive services may a state give to religious schools?

In a series of decisions the Supreme Court has attempted to draw a line between services that have discrete secular purposes and those that could be diverted to sectarian use. For example, the Court has found constitutional (1) psychological and speech diagnostic services by state personnel in private schools (a "public health service" that has "little or no educational content" thus reducing the chance of intrusion of sectarian views) and (2) therapeutic and remedial education services by state employees off the site of the religious school.[15] It has found unconstitutional (1) loans of instructional materials, including film projects, tape recorders, maps and globes, and similar items because of possible diversion to religious use and (2) reimbursement for field trips made at the discretion of school authorities who could make choices about destinations based on religious objectives. Following this "diversionary use" analysis, one federal court has recently upheld federal Chapter 2 funding for innovative educational services going to religious schools in the form of "self-monitoring" items such as "locked" computer software, books, and instructional materials selected by public school district staff.[16]

Can unrestricted maintenance and repair grants be given to religious elementary and secondary schools?

No. The Supreme Court rejected a New York program that gave such grants to schools because the primary effect of such payments would be the advancement of religion.[17] The Court found it impossible in these "pervasively sectarian" atmospheres to determine the nature of the use of such funds.

Can states reimburse religious schools for the costs of preparing tests mandated by state law?

The Supreme Court has drawn distinctions between the kinds of test costs that may be reimbursed. On one hand, it declared unconstitutional any reimbursement of traditional teacher-prepared tests, including those that measure student progress in subjects required by state law. The Court reasoned that simply because something is mandated by the state does not mean that it can be paid through public funding. Here, "despite the obviously integral role of such testing in the total teaching process, no attempt is made under the statute, and no means are available, to assure that internally prepared tests are free of religious instruction."[18] On the other hand, the Supreme Court has approved several programs in which testing and reporting for state-required *standardized* tests have been paid for by public funds, because the private-school had no control over the content of the tests. A New York program was found acceptable where such multiple-choice tests were graded by private-school teachers, because the Court found such scoring created no substantial risk that the exams could be used for purposes of religious education. The dissent argued that the level of reimbursement (ranging from 1 to 5.4 percent of a school's personnel budget) was a direct and substantial financial payment to a religious school.[19]

Can federal funds be used for the instruction of educationally deprived students who attend religious schools?

In the case *Aguilar v. Felton*, the Supreme Court ruled 5 to 4 that New York could not use so-called Chapter 1 federal funds to pay salaries of public employees who would teach remedial programs in religious school facilities.[20] The principal concern was the "excessive entanglement" caused by the need to verify that these teachers were not being influenced by their supervisors or surroundings to participate in religious education or other religious activities. In response, the U.S. Department of Education issued regulations that permitted the purchase of vans, essentially mobile classrooms, in which these services could be provided outside of the religious school building. The regulations also provided that in order to meet the statutory mandate of "equal expenditures" to students in private and public schools, any "administrative costs" (including the purchase of the vans) must come "off the top" of a state's overall allotment of federal funds.

A number of cases challenged these regulations. The city of Chicago, for example, argued unsuccessfully that the "administrative costs" actually benefit religious schools only and should be treated as a part of the overall support for students in religious schools. A federal appeals court rejected the argument, noting that "we do not believe that disparity in costs in the delivery of constitutionally permissible services render the program unconstitutional."[21] It added: "The cost of compliance with *Felton* is hardly a cost attributable to the children whose parents have exercised their constitutional right to send their child to a sectarian institution."

Several other federal appeals courts have also rejected constitutional arguments against "off the top" funding, maintaining that the disparate benefit to religious schools does not violate the Constitution,[22] and that even if "grossly disproportionate" the funding difference is too small to violate the Establishment

Clause (2.7 percent of total funds in one state). These latter decisions have rested on authority holding that the law requires only "comparable services," not identical ones, to all students.[23]

A second line of cases focused on where these mobile classrooms could be located. As of this writing, courts differ about whether a van can be parked on a religious school's property. One court has ruled that regardless of whether the van is located on public property near the school or on-site at the school, the "services are provided in a religiously neutral atmosphere and the units do not operate as 'annexes' of the parochial schools." This is buttressed by the fact that vans are driven away after use and that there is no "symbolic union" of church and state where the children leave their school to go to a new teacher in a new setting anywhere outside the school building.[24] Another court, however, has endorsed an off-premise/on-premise line on the rationale that parking vans on school property creates the impression of an impermissible symbolic union— that both the children and the public would assume the activity to be a cooperative effort of a religious group and the government.[25]

Can public school employees teach secular subjects in classrooms located in and leased from the nonpublic schools?

Programs sending state teachers into private schools to teach "supplemental" secular courses (those not required by state law) during the school day and those in which private-school teachers are paid for after-school secular "community education" classes are unconstitutional.[26] The Supreme Court majority found that both approaches impermissibly advance religion by forging a "symbolic union between government and religion in one sectarian enterprise" and by "taking over a substantial portion of [the religious schools'] responsibility for teaching secular subjects." With the teaching during the school day the Court feared that "teachers in such an atmosphere may well subtly (or overtly) conform their instruction to the environment in which they teach, while students will perceive the instruction provided in the context of dominating religious message of the institution, thus reinforcing the indoctrinating effect."[27] The after-school program posed "a substantial risk that, overtly or subtly, the religious messages they are expected to convey during the regular school day will enforce the supposedly secular classes they teach after school."[28]

Can states reimburse religiously affiliated colleges for instructing eligible advanced high school students?

Under a Minnesota law, juniors and seniors in high school could take courses for credit at local post-secondary institutions. A federal court ruled that since the institutions being reimbursed were not "pervasively sectarian" and the eligible courses had to be "nonsectarian," there was no First Amendment violation.[29]

Can government-subsidized programs place workers in religious schools?

Probably not, although few programs raise this issue. The Comprehensive Employment Training Act (CETA) was a federal program to provide economically disadvantaged persons with transitional employment in public service areas to develop job skills. Some CETA workers were placed in a variety of positions, including instructional summer jobs, custodial child care, nursing, and kitchen help in schools run by the Catholic Archdiocese of Milwaukee, Wisconsin. A court found many of the positions involving instruction or counseling to raise constitutional problems because of the possibility of government employees promoting religious values and the entanglement problem of deciding which instruction was purely secular.

Although kitchen and transportation helpers did not present these problems, the court ruled that "all placement of CETA workers in sectarian schools is prohibited under the Constitution because the structure of decision making about funding creates an impermissible risk of political entanglement for the CETA program as a whole."[30] This risk was particularly troublesome given the large amount of money involved and potential for political and religious competition.

In another case, a state university had permitted student teachers to fulfill student teaching requirements in parochial schools. This was also found unconstitutional because the "pervasively sectarian" nature of the schools meant that the "policy impermissibly advances religion by creating a perception that the state endorses the institution's religious mission."[31] The religious school benefited through the reimbursement of essentially unrestricted funds. The school also benefited by being able to evaluate the student teachers for future employment, thus ensuring conformity with the religiously based curriculum. The Court considered irrelevant that only students who chose to work in these schools were assigned there.

May states provide federally funded aid to the disabled attending religious schools?

The Supreme Court has held that under the Education of All Handicapped Children Act, funds can be used to pay for a signing interpreter to work with an eligible hearing-impaired student at a sectarian school. In *Zobrest v. Catalina Foothills School District*, the Court pointed out that the interpreter was provided as part of a general program available to all handicapped children and that the interpreter did nothing more than report what was said by others. The decision was a narrow one and probably does not foreshadow any general loosening of the restrictions on aid to parochial schools, even within the context of remedial education or services to the handicapped.[32] Thus, the Court did not overrule decisions that prohibited the placement of remedial instructors in the parochial schools.[33]

Can tuition reimbursements and other tax benefits be paid to parents whose children attend religious schools?

Probably not. The Supreme Court has ruled that even though the reimbursement funds went to parents instead of directly to the religious schools, the substantial effect was the same, the advancement of religion through a government subsidy.[34] In the same case, the Court also found a system of allowing parents to deduct from the aggregate gross income reported on state tax forms a portion of payments for private school tuition unconstitutional. This served as a "form of encouragement and reward for sending . . . children to nonpublic schools."[35] By a 5-to-4 margin, however, the Court upheld a Minnesota scheme in which parents of children attending public or private schools could deduct from their gross income a percentage of actual expenses for tuition, textbooks, and transportation.[36] The majority, giving broad deference to "classifications and distinctions in tax statutes," felt that this program "neutrally provides state assistance to a broad spectrum of citizens." Moreover, it concluded that the "public funds become available [to religious schools] only as a result of numerous, private choices of individual parents of school age children." The majority noted that unlike the earlier case where the tax benefit was available only to private-school parents, this program was open to all. (The four dissenting justices saw no significance to this distinction and labeled the Minnesota program "a financial incentive to send . . . children to sectarian schools" that directly benefited those schools. Moreover, since public school parents incur virtually no costs, the overwhelming benefit was to private schools—95 percent of which were religious.)

A few other courts have upheld similar tax deduction and tax credit arrangements, particularly where the state law expressly permitted the deduction (for parents with children in religious schools) only for the portion of expenses not attributable to religious instruction at these schools.[37]

Can government funds be used to construct buildings and other facilities at church-related colleges?

Yes, if it is clear that the construction is for facilities that will not be used for sectarian instruction or for religious worship. The Supreme Court upheld aid under the Higher Education Facilities Act, which contained such a prohibition on use, and agreed that at the four institutions where grants were challenged there was no evidence of worship services or religious symbols in constructed buildings.[38] The Court would not make the assumption that in such institutions of higher education religion would penetrate all of the secular educational programs, particularly since college-age students are "less impressionable and less susceptible to religious indoctrination" than younger students. The Court also found little chance of "excessive entanglement" in these one-time loans, arguing that "[s]uch inspection as may be necessary to ascertain that the facilities are devoted to secular education is minimal." It did hold a provision that would effectively permit use of a building for religious purposes after twenty years an Establishment Clause violation, concluding that the restriction could not expire when the building still had "substantial value." In a similar case, the Supreme Court also found no constitutional violation in South Carolina's issuance of revenue bonds that would benefit construction at state colleges and universities, including religiously affiliated ones. The Court found that the beneficiaries were not "pervasively sectarian" and that since the statute specifically excluded use of funds for places of worship or sectarian instruction, there was no primary effect of advancing religion. Moreover, a simple inspection, not ongoing surveillance, would determine whether the use of funds was proper.[39]

Can public funds be given to religiously affiliated colleges for general operating purposes?

Yes. The Supreme Court upheld a Maryland program of noncategorical grants to private colleges that specifically excluded use of the funds for "sectarian purposes."[40] The schools at issue, although religiously affiliated, were found not to be "pervasively sectarian." The Court refused to find "excessive entanglement" in the program. It did not believe that constant scrutiny would be required to determine that only secular activities were funded because of the reduced risk at a college that the study of history, the learning of a foreign language, or an athletic event will actually be infused with religious content or significance.[41] Moreover, the need for annual appropriations requests was not "any more entangling than the inspections and audits incidental to the normal process of the colleges' accreditation by the state."

One court has found an amendment to a general state tuition assistance grant program to be unconstitutional because it permitted funding for schools accredited by "the accrediting association of Bible colleges." Although the court was disturbed that the legislature had not specified which accrediting agency was appropriate, it also found that the unrestricted aid was going to sectarian schools "operated for express religious purposes" (and requiring attendance at worship and heavily weighing religious beliefs in student and faculty selection).[42]

Does the First Amendment bar tuition assistance for persons preparing to be a minister?

Generally yes, but there is an exception. The Supreme Court found no First Amendment problem where a state vocational rehabilitation assistance program expended funds for a blind resident to attend a Christian college in preparation for the ministry.[43] This narrowly drawn decision held that because the student was otherwise entitled to the funds due to his disability

and the funds were available for his or her discretionary use,
"any aid that ultimately flows to religious institutions does so
only as the result of the genuinely independent and private
choices of aid recipients" and is not "skewed toward religion."
The Court found that the program created no "financial incentive for students to undertake sectarian education." There was
also no evidence that "any significant portion of the aid . . .
will end up flowing to religious education" since the plaintiff
was the only person who ever sought money for this use.
Ironically, when the Supreme Court sent this back to Washington state courts, the student was denied benefits under the
state constitution.[44]

**Can tax dollars be used to fund religious activities in other
countries?**

For many years, schools in foreign nations were funded by
or sponsored by the United States through the American
Schools and Hospitals Abroad Program. The federal program
was interested in involving United States-based organizations
in assisting developing nations to build up their economic,
political, and social structures to improve the quality of life.
Some of the schools, however, were heavily dominated by
religious institutions. The federal appeals court reviewing
whether some of these grants violated the Establishment
Clause held that any constitutional violation would occur at
the time money was granted to the sponsoring United States-
based organizations, suggesting that even if all the money went
abroad, "because religion transcends national boundaries,
ASHA aid to a Catholic school in the Philippines may
strengthen not only that school, but also the Catholic Church
worldwide, and, in particular, the Catholic sponsor in the
United States and its domestic constituency."[45]

The court also rejected the claim that this program was
immune from scrutiny because of the foreign policy implica-
tions of support for these developing nations, concluding that
Establishment Clause standards would be flexible enough to
accommodate any "urgent dictates of United States foreign
policy."

When it sent this case back to a lower court for review of
the nature of the specific schools receiving the aid, it advised
that even if a school was "pervasively sectarian," "the govern-

ment should be permitted to demonstrate some compelling reason why the usually unacceptable risk attendant on funding such an institution should, in this particular case, be acceptable, as where a sectarian group is the only available channel for foreign aid or where no secular educational system even exists in a particular country.

Tax Exemption

Virtually all federal, state, and local taxes provide exemptions for religious institutions. Do such exemptions violate the Establishment Clause?

Most tax exemptions apply to both religious and secular nonprofit organizations and have been held not to violate the Establishment Clause.[46] However, those exemptions that are provided solely for religious institutions or religious publications and do not lift genuine burdens on religious exercise may violate the Establishment Clause. For example, the Supreme Court in *Texas Monthly v. Bullock*[47] held that a sales tax exemption provided solely for religious publications violated the Establishment Clause. According to the plurality opinion, "Every tax exemption constitutes a subsidy that affects nonqualifying taxpayers, forcing them to become 'indirect and vicarious donors. . . . [W]hen government directs a subsidy exclusively to religious organizations that is not required by the Free Exercise Clause and that either burdens nonbeneficiaries markedly or cannot reasonably be seen as removing a significant state-imposed deterrent to the free exercise of religion, . . . it 'provides unjustifiable awards of assistance to religious organizations' and cannot but 'convey a message of endorsement' to slighted members of the community."[48]

Are tax exemptions for religious organizations constitutionally required?

In the 1983 decision *Bob Jones University v. United States*,[49] the Supreme Court upheld the revocation of exemption from a university that prohibited interracial dating. Though the Court noted that the decision applied only to religious colleges and universities and not to churches and synagogues, Bob Jones University was a pervasively sectarian organization. More recently, in *Jimmy Swaggart Ministries v. Board of Equaliza-tion*,[50] the Supreme Court upheld the application of a sales-and-use tax to what was the equivalent of a church. The Court distinguishes its earlier decisions in *Murdock v. Pennsylvania*[51] and *Follett v. McCormick*[52] by limiting the holdings in those cases to flat license taxes that operate as a prior restraint on the exercise of religion. Justice O'Connor, speaking for the unanimous Court, stated that "the tax at issue in [*Swaggart*] is akin to a generally applicable income or property tax, which *Murdock* and *Follett* specifically state may constitutionally be imposed on religious activity."[53] Justice O'Connor did concede that it is possible "to imagine that a more onerous tax rate, even if generally applicable, might effectively choke off an adherent's religious practices" and therefore violate the Free Exercise Clause.[54]

Swaggart and *Bob Jones University*, coupled with the Court's broader holding in *Employment Division v. Smith*[55] that facially neutral, generally applicable laws not targeted at religion do not violate the Free Exercise Clause, suggest that tax exemption for religious organizations is not constitutionally required unless the tax imposes a particularly heavy burden on religion.

NOTES

1. *Foremaster v. City of St. George*, 882 F.2d 1485 (10th Cir. 1989).
2. *Bradfield v. Roberts*, 175 U.S. 291 (1899).
3. Some federal programs such as Medicare and Medicaid contain specific provisions that permit an aid recipient to choose among hospitals, including church-affiliated hospitals. In addition, although the Hill-Burton Act, which subsidizes hospital construction, generally prohibits construction that does not have a secular use, it specifically permits construction of "retiring rooms" in general hospitals for meditation and prayer and construction of chapels and related religious support in mental institutions. *See* discussion in Esbeck, *Government Regulation of Religiously Based Social Services: The First Amendment Considerations*, 19 Hastings Const. L.Q. 343 (1992). Although a number of state supreme courts, including those in Kentucky and Mississippi, have also ruled that the construction funds may be used for religious hospitals without violating their state constitutions, there is an occasional holding that a state cannot provide funding for a hospital owned

by a religious group (*see, e.g., Board of County Commissioners v. Idaho Health Facilities Authority*, 96 Idaho 498, 531 P.2d 588 (1974)).

4. *Bowen v. Kendrick*, 487 U.S. 589 (1988).

5. *Id.* at 641.

6. *Bob Jones University v. United States*, 461 U.S. 574, 604 (1983).

7. *Chrisman v. Sisters of St. Joseph of Peace*, 506 F.2d 308 (9th Cir. 1974) and *Taylor v. St. Vincent's Hospital*, 523 F.2d 75 (9th Cir. 1975), *cert. denied*, 424 U.S. 948 (1976).

8. *Everson v. Board of Education*, 330 U.S. 1 (1947).

9. *Id.* at 18.

10. *Id.* at 17.

11. *Members of Jamestown School Comm. v. Schmidt*, 699 F.2d 1 (1st Cir. 1983).

12. *Board of Education v. Allen*, 392 U.S. 236 (1968).

13. It should be noted that some state constitutions prohibit the provision of textbooks for and/or transportation to children attending parochial schools (*see* chapter 3).

14. *Lemon v. Kurtzman*, 403 U.S. 602 (1971).

15. *Wolman v. Walter*, 433 U.S. 229 (1977).

16. *Walker v. San Francisco Unified School Dist.*, 741 F. Supp. 1386 (N.D. Ca. 1990).

17. *Pearl v. Nyquist*, 413 U.S. 756 (1973).

18. *Levitt v. Comm. for Public Education and Religious Liberty*, 413 U.S. 472 (1973).

19. *PEARL v. Regan*, 444 U.S. 646 (1980); *see also Wolman v. Walter*, 433 U.S. 229 (1977).

20. *Aguilar v. Felton*, 473 U.S. 402 (1985).

21. *Board of Education for City of Chicago v. Alexander*, 983 F.2d 745 (7th Cir. 1992); *see also Walker v. San Francisco Unified School District*, 761 F. Supp. 1463 (N.D. Ca. 1991).

22. *Pulido v. Cavazos*, 934 F.2d 912 (8th Cir. 1991).

23. *Barnes v. Cavazos*, 966 F.2d 1056 (6th Cir. 1992).

24. *Pulido v. Cavazos, supra*, note 22.

25. *Walker v. San Francisco Unified School District*, 761 F. Supp. 1463 (N.D. Ca. 1991).

26. *Grand Rapids v. Ball*, 473 U.S. 374 (1985).

27. *Id.* at 397.

28. *Id.* at 387.

29. *Minnesota Federation of Teachers v. Nelson*, 740 F. Supp. 694 (D. Minn. 1990).

30. *Decker v. O'Donnell*, 661 F.2d 598, 615 (7th Cir. 1980).

31. *Stark v. St. Cloud State University*, 802 F.2d 1046 (8th Cir. 1986).

32. *Zobrest v. Catalina Foothills School District*, 113 S. Ct. 2462 (1993).

33. *Aguilar v. Felton*, 473 U.S. 402 (1985).
34. *Nyquist*, 413 U.S. 756 (1973).
35. *Id.* at 791.
36. *Mueller v. Allen*, 463 U.S. 388 (1983).
37. *Luthers v. Bair*, 788 F. Supp. 1032 (S.D. Iowa, 1992).
38. *Tilton v. Richardson*, 403 U.S. 672 (1971).
39. *Hunt v. McNair*, 413 U.S. 734 (1973).
40. *Roemer v. Bd. of Public Works*, 426 U.S. 736 (1976).
41. *Id.* at 762.
42. *d'Enrico v. Lesmeister*, 570 F. Supp. 158 (D.N.D. 1983).
43. *Witters v. Wash. Dept. of Services for the Blind*, 474 U.S. 481 (1986).
44. *Witters v. State Com'n for the Blind*, 771 P.2d 1119 (Wash. 1989).
45. *Lamont v. Woods*, 948 F.2d 825 (2d Cir. 1991).
46. *Walz v. Tax Commission*, 397 U.S. 664 (1970).
47. 489 U.S. 1 (1989).
48. *Bullock, supra* at 899–90 (citations omitted).
49. 461 U.S. 574 (1983).
50. 493 U.S. 378, 110 S. Ct. 688 (1990).
51. 319 U.S. 105 (1943).
52. 321 U.S. 573 (1944).
53. *Swaggart, supra* at 696.
54. *Swaggart, supra* at 697.
55. 494 U.S. 872 (1990).

IV

Religious Displays

May religious services occur on government property?

Yes, as long as no extraordinary effort or expense is incurred by a government entity, and there is no likelihood it will appear that the government is sponsoring the religious activity.

During Pope John Paul II's trip to the United States in the late 1970s, a challenge was raised to the use of federal funds to provide space and support for a Mass to be held on the National Mall in Washington. A federal appeals court found no First Amendment violation because the provision of police, barricades, and utilities was similar to that provided for a vast array of other large gatherings at this site. Given the range of speech activity that occurred in this "public forum" there was little chance anyone would conclude that this support constituted an endorsement of Catholicism. The Court noted that the archdiocese had itself spent $400,000 to erect a special platform and altar.[1]

However, on the same trip Pope John also visited Philadelphia, Pennsylvania. There, the city itself erected an altar and cross for the planned Mass at a cost of more than $200,000. The federal appeals court found this practice a clear First Amendment violation. "The city's assistance had effectively enabled the Pope to reach large numbers of persons and to perform a religious service. . . . He brought a religious message, with the help of the city, from the Roman Catholic Church to millions of persons. This is an effect that can only be considered as advancing religion." The court also found "excessive entanglement" in the joint efforts between the city and the archdiocese in deciding platform design, ticket distribution, policing, and numerous other matters.[2]

In another case, a federal appeals court stopped a Mass from being conducted as part of a city-sponsored Italian Festival in a public park.[3] There was agreement that if the event had been a privately sponsored one, no violation would have occurred. Here, though, the "religious service under governmental auspices necessarily conveys the message of approval or endorsement . . . even when the endorsement takes place in company with secular events, such as the food, crafts, and entertainment offered at the Festival." The Court noted that a city employee had actually recruited the priest and that a city brochure advertised an "Italian Mass to be celebrated at our Italian Festival."

Can a city include a Nativity scene in an "official" Christmas display on privately owned property?

In the closely decided case of *Lynch v. Donnelly*, five justices ruled that inclusion of a Nativity scene in the city-owned display of Christmas imagery (including a Santa Claus house, candy-striped poles, Christmas trees, reindeer, teddy bears, and a "Season's Greetings" banner) in a privately owned park did not violate the Establishment Clause.[4] The four dissenting justices applied the standard *Lemon* analysis. The majority found that the display had the secular purpose of "celebrating the Holiday" and bringing shoppers downtown; it was only an indirect, remote, and incidental benefit to the advancement of religion; and there was no entanglement between the city and any religious body. Justice O'Connor concurred with the result but articulated her endorsement test (discussed in chapter I) and argued that the display simply did not communicate a message that the government endorsed the Christian beliefs represented by the crèche.

Five years after the *Lynch* case, the Supreme Court took a look at two holiday displays in Pittsburgh, Pennsylvania.[5] The first was a Nativity scene on the Grand Staircase of the Allegheny County Courthouse, donated by a private group and containing a sign indicating its source. (These notices are generally referred to as "disclaimers," which purport to inform viewers of the true ownership of the display.) The second was an eighteen-foot-tall Hanukkah menorah (candelabra) just outside the City-County Building near a decorated Christmas tree and a sign indicating the overall display was a "salute to liberty."

Using the endorsement test articulated by Justice O'Connor in *Lynch* as a refinement of previous analysis in these cases, the Court majority found that by displaying the solitary Nativity scene inside the courthouse "the county sends an unmistakable message that it supports and promotes the Christian praise to God that is the crèche's religious message" and constituted "the government's lending its support to the communication of a religious organization's religious message."[6]

On the other hand, a majority did not find "endorsement" in the menorah display. The Court held that the menorah was part of a larger holiday display containing secular symbols. In addition, several justices felt the menorah was no longer "exclusively religious" because of its additional cultural meaning and significance. Indeed, these justices suggested it would be discriminatory against Jews to allow the celebration of Christmas as a cultural tradition (with a Christmas tree) while not acknowledging Chanukah as a similar tradition.[7] (Justice O'Connor herself reached the same conclusion but not because the menorah had become a secular symbol. Rather, she noted that in this context it helped "convey its own distinctive message of pluralism and freedom of belief during the holiday season.") The conclusion of the majority was that it would not be "significantly likely" that the "reasonable observer" would take the overall display as approval of a religious choice.

The results in these cases set out the Supreme Court's tests for determining whether state sponsorship of a temporary religious symbol amounted to an establishment of religion. However, because erecting religious symbols is a form of free speech, the courts have had to consider whether denying private groups access to a particular public space denies them freedom of speech. In such cases, the courts must decide whether permitting the speech (thus protecting freedom of speech) would suggest impermissible governmental endorsement of religion.

Can a city permit private religious holiday displays on government property?

In several cases, freestanding religious symbols close to or in government buildings have been found unconstitutional. The federal Court of Appeals for the Fourth Circuit found a local government's grant of permission to the Jaycees to place a Nativity scene on the front lawn of the county office building unconstitutional because "one could not readily view the crèche without also viewing the trapping and identifying marks of the state."[8] Even though the lawn had been used sporadically and might even be a "public forum" (a place open to a wide variety of speeches and other activities) the "associational message" was still strong enough to trigger an Establishment Clause violation.

The Second Circuit also ruled unconstitutional a solitary menorah owned by a private group but displayed in a park in front of a Vermont City Hall.[9] It found the menorah a clearly religious symbol when standing alone (a factor emphasized because in prior years its candles were lit in a religious ceremony) and when displayed in an area "closely associated with a core government function" an endorsement of religion. This court noted that the park was not a "public forum" for "unattended religious displays" and that even if it were so construed, its characterization as a "public forum" is just one factor to consider in determining whether "the context of the display suggests government endorsement."

However, the Eleventh Circuit held the state of Georgia could not deny the placement of a freestanding menorah in the rotunda of the state capitol.[10] Because the area had been used by private groups in the past, the Establishment Clause was not a "compelling state interest" justifying the menorah's exclusion. The fact that this area was a "public forum" meant that visitors would be aware of past activity and would not conclude that the menorah occupies the center of the capitol with the support and approval of the state of Georgia.[11]

As one moves further from government buildings or adds elements to the display, courts have been more willing to find a display permissible. The Sixth Circuit has found a Nativity scene on a city hall front lawn constitutionally permissible because it was included with a variety of secular items that "detracted from the crèche's religious message." Conceding that the location was problematic, it nevertheless felt the display sent a "message of pluralism" and did not "convey an endorsement of Christianity."[12] The same circuit found no constitutional violation where Kentucky erected—after receiving private funds to cover the cost—a "rustic stable" that did not contain Nativity scene figures on the capitol grounds but which was used by church groups to stage religious pageants.[13] Of particular significance to this court was that the area and the "stable" itself was designated with a disclaimer that it was not constructed with public funds and was specifically described on the disclaimer as a "public forum."

In a third case, the same appeals court allowed a privately

funded menorah display in Caldor Plaza of Grand Rapids, Michigan, a plaza that also includes city and county government buildings.[14] It concluded that since there was a visible disclaimer of any government involvement and a past history of use of this area for speeches and temporary structures, the "reasonable observer" would not conclude that Grand Rapids "endorses religion." (It noted that the only reason it stood alone was that no other group had elected to erect a structure of its own.)

The Second Circuit has also held that a village's accommodation of a crèche in a traditional public forum in a retail area was not an Establishment Clause violation, at least if an adequate disclaimer was present.[15] The logic of this court was expanded recently by the Ninth Circuit in permitting a private group to erect an eight-scene display of the life of Jesus in a park pavilion for six weeks.[16] Crucial factors there included the disclaimer sign, the pavilion's distance from any "trappings of government," that this "public forum" had not been closed to other large, unattended displays, and that the group had "non-exclusive" use of the pavilion (with the scenes draped when it was used by others).

Can governmental entities themselves erect or maintain permanent religious symbols on public property?

In general, courts around the country have found the permanent display on public lands of particular symbols, such as a Latin cross or the Star of David, as violations of the Establishment Clause if they are maintained by government entities. Each court tends to focus on slightly different issues because of the unique placement of these objects. The cases discussed here are illustrative.

A federal court found that the construction (later reimbursed with private funds) and maintenance of three crosses and the Star of David in a Houston, Texas, park was intended to be a religious "meditation" area, with a primarily religious effect: "These permanent symbols become state symbols when placed in a public park, and they convey purely religious messages," indeed religious messages of only two particular faiths.[17] This court specifically rejected the argument that removing the symbols would amount to the establishment of "Humanism" as the government's religion.

Even where the symbol has a nonreligious purpose, such as memorializing war veterans, the overwhelmingly religious character of the symbol generally makes their maintenance unconstitutional. A large cross at a Marine base in Hawaii was ordered removed because a war memorial could have been erected without "the needless use of means that are inherently religious" that made "a message of endorsement likely if not unavoidable." This court also noted that the cross had caused considerable political divisiveness.[18]

Embracing tourism has also been rejected as a sufficient secular basis to overcome the clear religious message of an eighty-five-foot lighted cross in a state park, particularly where the cross was explicitly erected to meet an Easter Sunday deadline and had been endorsed by the mayor.[19]

The closer the connection between the cross or religious symbol and a government building or structure, the more likely that a violation will be found. Crosses on a city water tower (where it stood near a "Welcome to St. Cloud" sign)[20] and atop a city fire station[21] have also been found unconstitutional.

Some courts distinguish cases like those above and permit permanent crosses. In one case, the Knights of Columbus erected a crucifix as a war memorial in a publicly owned park. The court felt that the "average citizen would not believe that the Township's purpose was to advance or endorse Christianity," particularly because this park was far from any government buildings and was a "quintessential public forum." In its judgment, this was "private religious speech" and there was no evidence that the town denied others permission to erect similar structures. This decision was reversed on appeal.[22]

Similarly, a federal court in California found no violation caused by the mere presence (without any maintenance costs) of a large cross in a public park atop Mount Davidson.[23] This court felt that it could not be viewed as promoting religion because it was not on or near a government building, was not advertised or highlighted in official tourist literature and was in a "unique historical and physical setting" (allegedly built as a work of art and ceremoniously lit by President Franklin Roosevelt, it is now apparently hard to see from most of San Francisco because of cloud cover).

Also based on a "public forum" analysis, one federal appeals court has permitted the erection of a sixteen-painting depiction of the life of Jesus in a city park, three blocks from City Hall in Ottawa, Illinois.[24] The court opined that "the mere presence of religious symbols in a public forum does not violate the Establishment Clause, since the government is not presumed to endorse every speaker that it fails to censor in a quintessential public forum far removed from the seats of government."

Where the symbol is less obviously religious, there is less likelihood of a First Amendment violation. One court found that a Memorial to the Unknown Child erected on city property near a Catholic church by a group associated with that body was not unconstitutional notwithstanding an overtly religious (and anti-abortion) dedication ceremony and a rancorous city council vote to permit its continuance that occurred along religious lines.[25] The court concluded that even if it were an anti-abortion "statement," the fact that such a point of view coincided with the doctrine of the Roman Catholic Church behind it would not render it unconstitutional.

Do state constitutions create independent grounds for finding religious symbols unconstitutional?

In some cases they may, but the only significant litigation on this matter has occurred in California. The California Constitution contains two specific provisions that differ from the provisions of the U.S. Constitution. One provides that the state may not discriminate between religions or prefer one religion over another.[26] A second strictly prohibits any governmental support for religious purposes.[27] The California state courts have interpreted these provisions as being more comprehensive than the federal counterparts.[28]

A federal appeals court first applied these provisions to a religious display case involving the ownership by San Bernadino County of a small park with a collection of biblical statuary that had been donated to the county by the sculptor at his death. This court reasoned that unlike a museum, where religious paintings or objects may be displayed along with other kinds of material, this park is "restricted to only the artwork already in existence." Moreover, the religious nature of the statues is actually emphasized by the proximity of the park to a church and a hillside cross. The court labeled this "a statue collection of Christian symbols displayed and maintained by the government." Combined with the past involvement of the county with the park that included producing a promotional brochure that contained religious messages, this gave the appearance of government endorsement. Therefore, even though the park served a secular purpose of attracting tourists, the provisions of the state constitution do not permit "use of a religious statutory park to achieve a secular goal."[29]

Applying these principles to several other controversies, the same court found the display of crosses unlawful under the state constitution.[30] One was a thirty-six-foot cross on a three-acre parcel highly visible in the San Diego Hills that had been deeded to the city. The other was a privately erected forty-three-foot cross on a city-owned parcel of land. The court held that, when a symbol (1) is located on public property, (2) has obvious religious significance to a particular religion, (3) is of considerable magnitude and visibility, (4) does not include display of other religious symbols or objects to "neutralize" it, and (5) lacks historical significance independent of its religious content, it is likely to create a prohibited appearance of religious preference.

Can government seals or insignias incorporate religious symbols?

In most cases, courts have found the inclusion of overtly religious symbols in city and county seals and insignia to violate the Establishment Clause. As with the cross cases discussed above, these decisions tend to turn on the particular facts in the case.

In Bernalillo County, New Mexico, the official seal contained a Latin cross and the phrase *Con Esta Vencemos* (With This We Conquer). The symbol pervaded the daily life of the community from official stationery to police uniforms and cars. A federal appeals court found that this constituted an advancement of religion through an "implicit symbolic benefit": "The seal as used conveys a strong impression to the average observer that Christianity is being endorsed. It recalls a less tolerant time and foreshadows its return. Religious minorities may not be made to feel like outsiders because of government's malicious or merely unenlightened endorsement of the majority faith."[31] The court noted that a person approached by a patrol car with this seal "could reasonably assume that the officers were Christian police."

Another federal appeals court found constitutional violations in two Illinois city seals.[32] The first, in Rolling Meadows, was created by an eighth grade student who drew a four-leaf clover design with four representations of things she saw from her house, including a leaf, a school, some industrial buildings, and a church with a cross being constructed in her neighborhood. This court found this "permanent statement that is viewed year round" containing a "conspicuous depiction of the pre-eminent symbol of a particular faith" to convey "a message of approval that is simply inconsistent with the First Amendment." It observed: "To any observer. . . the seal expresses the City's approval of these four pictures of city-life its flora, its schools, its industry and commercial life and its Christianity."[33]

It was even easier to find a violation in the city seal of Zion, Illinois, where the town had been founded as a religious city by the Catholic Christian Church. The founder had created the seal, complete with a ribbon with the phrase "God Reigns" and four other symbols (a dove, a cross, a sword, and a crown) explicitly chosen for their religious significance to his faith. Not only did the seal design have religious origins, it would "create an unmistakable impression that the local government tacitly endorses Christianity." The court rejected the argument that the "historical significance" of the design prevented a finding of unconstitutionality.

In a third case, however, a federal appellate court accepted a historical argument and held that the inclusion of a cross in the insignia of Austin, Texas, did not violate the First Amendment.[34] The cross had been part of the coat of arms of the city's founder and was a relatively small part of the overall seal design which contained other secular elements. This seal was held not to "demonstrate a preference for Christianity" because of "a long standing unique history, absolutely no evidence of an intent to proselytize, or advance, any religion, and no threat of an establishment of religion."[35]

May a government allow a religious group to erect nonsymbolic devices necessary for the accommodation of their religious beliefs?

One district court has considered the creation of an *eruv* by a Jewish congregation not to violate the Establishment Clause. An *eruv* is an unbroken delineation of an area that would permit otherwise prohibited activities such as pushing a baby carriage and carrying to occur in that space on the Jewish Sabbath. The congregation strung wires between utility poles and fences and erected a few new poles to accomplish the job.

The court found that the *eruv* is not a religious symbol and that the town had a legitimate secular purpose in allowing a large group of citizens increased access to public properties, on an equal basis with people of other backgrounds. Since the *eruv* was barely noticeable and conveyed no religious message, the court found no reason to believe any reasonable person would feel the city had put its imprimatur on religious activity.[36]

May a government lease public space to religious organizations?

It appears that courts will uphold the right to lease public property on a nondiscriminatory basis to religious groups if it has done so for other secular organizations, although no cases suggest that any preferential treatment is required or, indeed, would be permitted.

As one example, the San Francisco Airport Authority had decided not to lease airport space to "religious groups" and thus decided not to renew the lease for a Christian Science Reading Room. A federal appeals court found this action unconstitutional and lacking any legitimate state purpose.[37] It concluded that there was "nothing to suggest that the airport endorsed the religious views and beliefs of the reading room or gave favored status to religion in general simply by allowing the reading room to occupy leased space. This was seen as a simple commercial leasing arrangement to garner revenue, with the "benefits" of a lease open to anyone wanting to "hawk their wares." Moreover, the airport had never sought control over what was available at this location, so no entanglement with religion had occurred.

NOTES

1. *O'Hair v. Andrus*, 613 F.2d 931 (D.C. Cir. 1979).
2. *Gilfillan v. City of Philadelphia*, 637 F.2d 924 (3d Cir. 1980).
3. *Doe v. Crestwood*, 917 F.2d 1476 (7th Cir. 1990).
4. *Lynch v. Donnelly*, 465 U.S. 688 (1984).

5. *County of Allegheny v. ACLU*, 492 U.S. 573 (1989).

6. *Id.* at 600.

7. *Id.* at 615. *But see Lubavitch Chabad House v. Chicago*, 917 F.2d 341 (7th Cir. 1990). (Even where public area in airport had Christmas trees deemed secular, city was not obligated to permit erection of menorah by private group to avoid "religious discrimination.")

8. *Smith v. County of Albemarle*, 895 F.2d 953 (4th Cir. 1990) *cert. denied*, 111 S. Ct. 74 (1990); *see also ACLU v. County of Delaware*, 726 F. Supp. 184 (S.D. Ohio, 1989). (Nativity scene owned by county and erected on courthouse lawn "impermissibly endorses religion.")

9. *Kaplan v. City of Burlington*, 891 F.2d 1024 (2d Cir. 1989), *cert. denied*, 110 S. Ct. 2619 (1990).

10. *Chabad-Lubavitch of Georgia v. Miller*, 5 F.3d 1383 (11th Cir. 1993).

11. *Id.* at 1395.

12. *Doe v. City of Clausen*, 915 F.2d 244 (6th Cir. 1990).

13. *ACLU v. Wilkinson*, 895 F.2d 1098 (6th Cir. 1990).

14. *Americans United v. City of Grand Rapids*, 980 F.2d 1538 (6th Cir. 1992).

15. *McCreary v. Stone*, 739 F.2d 716 (2d Cir. 1984), *aff'd by an equally divided court*, 471 U.S. 83 (1985).

16. *Kreisner v. City of San Diego*, 988 F.2d 883 (9th Cir. 1993).

17. *Greater Houston Chapter of ACLU v. Eckels*, 589 F. Supp. 222 (1984).

18. *Jewish War Veterans v. U.S.*, 695 F. Supp. 3 (D.D.C. 1988).

19. *ACLU of Georgia v. Rabun County Chamber of Commerce*, 698 F.2d 1098 (11th Cir. 1983).

20. *Mendelsohn v. City of St. Cloud*, 719 F. Supp. 1065 (M.D. Fla. 1989).

21. *ACLU v. City of St. Charles*, 794 F.2d 265 (7th Cir. 1986), *cert. denied*, 479 U.S. 961 (1986).

22. *Gonzales v. North Twshp. of Lake County*, 800 F. Supp. 676 (N.D. Ind. 1992), rev'd, 4 F.3d 1412 (7th Cir. 1994).

23. *Carpenter v. City and County of San Francisco*, 803 F. Supp. 337 (N.D. Cal. 1992).

24. *Doe v. Small*, 964 F.2d 611 (7th Cir. 1992).

25. *Fausto v. Diamond*, 589 F. Supp. 451 (D.R.I. 1984).

26. Cal. Const. art. I, § 4 ("free exercise and enjoyment of religion without discrimination or preference").

27. Cal. Const. art. I, § 5.

28. *Fox v. City of Los Angeles*, 587 P.2d 663 (Cal. 1978) (holding that Los Angeles may not display a lighted cross on city hall).

29. *Hewitt v. Joyner*, 940 F.2d 1561 (9th Cir. 1991), *cert. denied*, 112 S. Ct. 969 (1992).

30. *Ellis v. City of La Mesa*, 990 F.2d 1518 (9th Cir. 1993).

31. *Friedman v. Board of County Com'rs of Bernalillo*, 781 F.2d 777, 782 (10th Cir. 1985), *cert. denied*, 426 U.S. 1169 (1986).
32. *Harris v. City of Zion*, 927 F.2d 1401 (7th Cir. 1991), *cert. denied*, 112 S. Ct. 3025 (1992).
33. *Id.* at 1412.
34. *Murray v. City of Austin*, 947 F.2d 147 (5th Cir. 1991), *cert. denied*, 112 S. Ct. 3028 (1992).
35. *Id.* at 155.
36. *ACLU v. City of Long Branch*, 670 F. Supp. 1293 (D.N.J. 1987).
37. *Christian Science Reading Room v. City of San Francisco*, 784 F.2d 1010 (9th Cir. 1986).

V

Chaplains

Can legislative bodies hire chaplains?

The Supreme Court has upheld the constitutionality of chaplains hired principally to provide prayers to open daily sessions of state legislatures.[1] The Court did not apply the traditional three-prong analysis of the *Lemon* test. Instead, it relied on "the unambiguous and unbroken history of more than 200 years" of opening legislative sessions, including those of Congress, with prayer, a practice it claimed "has become a part of the fabric of our society." The majority held that "[T]o invoke Divine guidance on a public body entrusted with making the laws . . . is simply a tolerable acknowledgment of beliefs widely held among the people of this country."[2] The Court specifically found that the lengthy and paid tenure of the current chaplain, a Presbyterian, "did not advance the belief of a particular church and demonstrated only that "his performance and personal qualities were acceptable to the body appointing him."

Several state courts have also upheld the practice of paid state chaplains against claims under their state constitutions.[3]

Can governments provide chaplains in the military or in prisons at taxpayers' expense?

Although there is no Supreme Court decision on this matter, there is little question that the United States government can provide chaplains for military personnel, both overseas and at home.[4] Similarly, public funding for chaplains in prisons has been repeatedly deemed constitutional.[5] Although often criticized, the theory is that persons who are in government institutions, voluntarily or involuntarily, are entitled to access to religious worship and counseling, and that this interest overrides any Establishment Clause problem.

In one interesting case, a federal district court ruled that Veterans Administration rules that chaplains be "ordained" violated the constitutional rights of those women who could not be "ordained" within their religious tradition.[6] This turned out to be a hollow victory for the plaintiff, however, since the court acknowledged that the V.A. could still require some kind of official "endorsement" by a denomination, and the Roman Catholic Church of which she was a member would not grant her such recognition. Thus, she was still not able to serve.

NOTES

1. *Marsh v. Chambers*, 463 U.S. 783 (1983).
2. *Id.* at 792.
3. *See, e.g., Colo. v. Treasurer and Receiver General*, 392 N.E. 2d 1195 (Mass. 1979).
4. *Katcoff v. Marsh*, 755 F.2d 233 (2d Cir. 1985).
5. *See, e.g., Rudd v. Ray*, 248 N.W. 2d 125 (Iowa 1976).
6. *Murphy v. Derwinski*, 776 F. Supp. 1466 (D. Colo. 1991), *aff'd*, 996 F.2d 540 (10th Cir. 1993).

VI
Religion and Family Law

Can religion be made an issue in child custody cases?

In general, the principal criterion for determining which parent obtains custody of a child after a divorce is the "best interest of the child."[1] Just what, if any, weight should be accorded the religious views of parents has been the subject of considerable differences of opinion between state courts. (The United States Supreme Court has chosen not to accept cases raising this issue.)

A few states have maintained that religion must play no role in custody hearings because to do so excessively entangles courts in religious matters.[2] Some other courts allow religion to be one of a multitude of general factors that can be considered. For example, a Pennsylvania decision holds that within the general "best interest" consideration is "the stability and consistency of the child's spiritual inculcation"—which requires a "review of their [the parents'] respective religious beliefs."[3]

The most common rule, however, is that only when specific religious beliefs or practices impede a child's development in some articulable way can custodial decisions be made on such a basis. Some courts allow such arguments before the custodial decision is granted;[4] others appear to apply such tests only in consideration of changing custody orders after evidence of "actual impairment of physical, emotional, and mental well being" has been demonstrated.[5]

The results under these differing—and admittedly vague—standards present real difficulty in locating generally applicable principles. The following cases illustrate some recent results and demonstrate the confusing state of the law on this issue.

For example, custody decisions have been made on the basis that one parent was a member of the Jehovah's Witnesses faith. A Minnesota court granted a change in custody to a father based in part on the religious practices of the Jehovah's witness mother, which included her opposition to the celebration of religious holidays and birthdays and discouragement of participation in school extracurricular activities.[6] On the other hand, the Ohio Supreme Court has ruled that a court could not give preference to a Catholic father over a mother who had become a convert to the Jehovah's Witnesses religion merely because the child would be prevented from flag saluting and dancing. "Evidence that the child will not be permitted to participate in certain social or patriotic activities is not sufficient to prove possible harm."[7]

In general, courts will not make custody decisions on the basis of religiously motivated choices about education or lifestyle. For example, an Ohio appeals court ruled that the trial court had erred in ordering a change in custody because the custodial parent was pursuing "home schooling" for her children, notwithstanding an expert witness's prediction of "eventual harm" from the chosen educational method.[8] Similarly, a Pennsylvania court also found trial court error where a change of custody was ordered because it felt a Christian fundamentalist father was raising his child in a "sterile" environment with a "singlehanded approach to life."[9] The appeals court felt that the trial judge had merely substituted his religious preferences for those of the father. On the other hand, the Missouri Supreme Court rested a custody decision on the conclusion that a parental belief that the child should not be permitted to attend any school that taught evolution would have a negative impact on the "child's development."[10]

Will a child's religious view be given consideration in custody proceedings?
If an older child has developed religious preferences and those are part of his or her identity, they are likely to be considered.[11] Most courts, however, are unlikely to give much weight to such preferences of preteen children.[12]

Can custody decisions be conditioned on changes in a parent's religious beliefs or practices?
Although there are few cases on this subject, it is probably not permissible to so condition custody grants. A Nebraska court would not condition custody on removing children from a private Christian school, notwithstanding evidence that the local public school facilities were superior.[13] Similarly, a Florida court refused to condition custody on severing all ties to a church alleged to practice "brainwashing."[14]

Can courts condition visitation rights for noncustodial parents on compliance with the custodial parent's religious wishes?

Again, it is difficult to draw clear conclusions from the patchwork of state court decisions in this area. For example, a Hindu father has been required to have his child attend Ukrainian Catholic Church masses, which the mother felt were necessary for the child's spiritual development.[15] Likewise, an appeals court has upheld a trial court order for a noncustodial parent not to involve a child in any Jehovah's Witnesses activities because they seemed to cause "stress" in the child.[16] An Arizona court prohibited a Jewish noncustodial parent from taking the child to religious instruction simply because the custodial parent objected.[17]

On the other hand, other courts refuse to become involved in noncustodial parents' religious activities, absent a very clear showing of harm to the child. One court ruled that a child's exposure to different religious "role models" is beneficial.[18] Some courts will not order noncustodial parents to fulfill religious obligations imposed by the custodial parent.[19]

Will courts uphold prenuptial agreements about religion?

Probably not. The Connecticut Supreme Court, for example, refused to uphold such an agreement that the children of a marriage would be raised in the faith of the father.[20] A Pennsylvania court specifically found that enforcing an agreement that a Catholic custodial parent could not take children to any non-Jewish religious service was legally unenforceable as "excessive entanglement" under the Establishment Clause.[21] That court did indicate, however, that a court could provide time for both parents to attempt to inculcate their religious beliefs. New York, however, will enforce a separation agreement that controls the religious upbringing of a child, subject to the court's power to abrogate the agreement in the best interest of the child.[22]

Can religious differences be grounds for divorce?

There are only occasional cases in which religion plays a role in a divorce proceeding. The Idaho Supreme Court has held that a wife's ridicule of her husband's religious belief could be grounds for divorce.[23]

May religion play a role in adoption or foster care placement decisions?

Almost all states will permit consideration of whether prospective adoptive parents have religious beliefs in an overall examination of fitness. In addition, many states have laws that mandate, or at least prefer, that wherever "practical," children put up for adoption or scheduled for placement in foster homes should end up in a home of the same religion as that of the children's biological parent. These laws developed from the general common law right of parents to control the religious upbringing and education of their children.

There is growing litigation, however, over the application of this principle. In one particularly controversial case, involving the placement of orphans airlifted to the U.S. before the fall of Cambodia to the Khmer Rouge, a California court found that the policy of the evangelical adoption service to place these children only with families who were members of evangelical Protestant churches violated the Establishment Clause. The court reasoned that any state-licensed agencies for adoption placement must be neutral in regard to religion and show no religious preference.[24] Other states have also found the use of religion as the sole determinant of placement to be unconstitutional.[25]

New York, which has a state constitutional provision for religious matching in foster home placements, also found itself in protracted litigation. The city of New York used public funds to place foster children in group homes, many run by religious organizations. After an initial ruling that this system did not violate the Establishment Clause on its face,[26] New York courts had to examine whether the effect of the policy was unconstitutional. A settlement was eventually reached in which, in general, children in need of foster care placement would be placed on a "first-come-first-served" basis without consideration of the religious preference of biological parents. The agencies receiving those children had to provide for religious observances in accordance with each child's religious beliefs, could not restrict access to city-funded abortion and contraceptive services, and could not have religious symbols displayed in a manner that would make a child placed in an agency home of a different religion feel coerced. When some Catholic and Jewish organizations objected to the conditions of this settlement and sued, a federal court upheld the conditions of the agreement.[27]

NOTES

1. *See generally* J. Atkinson, *Modern Child Custody Practice* (1986).
2. *See, e.g., Sanborn v. Sanborn*, 465 A.2d 888 (N.H. 1983).
3. *Morris v. Morris*, 412 A.2d 139 (Pa. Super. Ct. 1979).
4. *Clift v. Clift*, 346 So. 2d 429 (Ala. Ct. App. 1977).
5. *Quiner v. Quiner*, 59 Calif. Rptr. 503 (Calif. Ct. App. 1967).
6. *In re Marriage of Letterman v. Letterman*, (Minn. Ct. App. 1990); *see also* M. Tyner, "Who Gets the Kid?", *Liberty*, May/June 1991 (discussion of case in which decision in Florida was based on fact that child raised by Jehovah's Witnesses mother would not fit in American mainstream).
7. *Pater v. Pater*, 63 Ohio St.3d 393, 588 N.E. 2d 794 (Ohio 1992).
8. *Gardini v. Moyer*, (Ohio Ct. App. 1990).
9. *Stolarick v. Novak* (Pa. Super. Ct. 1991).
10. *Waites v. Waites*, 567 S.W. 2d 326 (Mo. 1978).
11. *Bonjour v. Bonjour*, 592 P.2d 1233 (Alaska 1979).
12. *See, e.g., Munoz v. Munoz*, 79 Wash. 2d 810, P.2d 1133 (1971) (*en banc*) (six-year-old too young to choose religion).
13. *Von Tersch v. Von Tersch*, 235 Neb. 263 (1990).
14. *Rogers v. Rogers*, 490 So. 2d 1017 (Fla. App. 1 Dist. 1986).
15. *Bryan v. Nayyar*, 572 N.Y.S.2d 821 (N.Y. App. Div. 1991).
16. *LeDoux v. LeDoux*, 452 N.W.2d 1 (Neb. 1990).
17. *Funk v. Ossman*, 150 Ariz. 578, 724 P.2d 1247 (Ariz. App. 1986).
18. *Felton v. Felton*, 383 Mass. 232, 418 N.E.2d 606 (1981).
19. *See, e.g., Matthews v. Matthews*, 273 S.C. 130, 254 S.E.2d 801 (1979).
20. *McLaughlin v. McLaughlin*, 132 A.2d 420 (Conn. 1957).
21. *Zummo v. Zummo*, 1720 Phila. 1988 (Pa. Super.).
22. *Spring v. Glawan*, 89 A.D.2d 980, 454 N.Y.S.2d 140 (App. Div., 2d Dept. 1982).
23. *Lepel v. Lepel*, 93 Idaho 82, 456 P.2d 249 (1969).
24. *Scott v. Family Ministries*, 135 Cal. Rptr. 430 (1976).
25. *See, e.g., In re Adoption of "E,"* 279 A.2d 785 (N.J. 1971); *Orzechowski v. Perales*, 582 N.Y.S. 2d 341 (N.Y. Sup. Ct. 1992).
26. *Wilder v. Sugarman*, 385 F. Supp. 1013 (S.D.N.Y. 1974).
27. *Wilder v. Bernstein*, 848 F.2d 1338 (2d Cir. 1988).

VII

The Free Exercise Clause

What is the purpose of the Free Exercise Clause?

As noted, the purpose of the Establishment Clause and the Free Exercise Clause is to guarantee religious liberty. The Free Exercise Clause seeks to accomplish this by forbidding Congress from passing laws prohibiting the free exercise of religion. The clause protects the rights of individuals and groups insofar as possible to practice their religion free from governmental interference.

Does the Free Exercise Clause apply to other branches of the federal government besides Congress?

Yes, the Free Exercise Clause restricts the legislative, executive, and judicial branches of government.[1]

What about state and local governments?

They, too, are subject to the restriction against laws prohibiting the free exercise of religion. The Due Process Clause of the Fourteenth Amendment has been interpreted as applying the Free Exercise Clause to state and local governments.[2]

Does the Free Exercise Clause forbid only laws that literally prohibit the free exercise of religion?

No. The clause has been interpreted by the courts as prohibiting laws that impose a substantial burden on religious exercise.[3] A law that required ministers to purchase a license in order to preach, for example, would almost certainly violate the Free Exercise Clause and the Free Speech Clause although the law did not prohibit preaching altogether.[4]

Is the right to practice one's religion absolute?

No. While the right to hold religious beliefs is absolute, the right to act on those beliefs is not.[5] The Supreme Court has recognized that the right to practice one's religion must yield to the interests of society in some circumstances. A parent's right to refuse medical treatment for a sick child, for example,

may be subordinate to the state's interest in protecting the
health, safety, and welfare of its minor children.[6] Similarly,
polygamy and child labor laws have been upheld in the face
of free exercise challenges.[7]

**Is a person's right to the free exercise of religion contingent
upon his or her membership in a recognized religious group?**
    No. The Free Exercise Clause protects the smallest and least
popular religious minorities. Even a minority of one is entitled
to the free exercise of religion.[8]

**Has the Supreme Court adopted a particular legal test
to assist in deciding cases arising under the Free Exercise
Clause?**
    The Court has adopted two irreconcilable standards. In the
1963 decision of *Sherbert v. Verner*,[9] the Supreme Court
adopted a four-part test for evaluating free exercise cases. Adele
Sherbert, an Adventist, had been denied unemployment compensation benefits for refusing to accept a job that would have
required her to work on her sabbath. The Supreme Court,
speaking through Justice William Brennan, held that Ms. Sherbert could not be forced to choose between her religious convictions and her government benefits. Such a "cruel choice," said
the Court, was a violation of the Free Exercise Clause.
    Almost a decade later, the Court overturned the conviction
of Jonas Yoder, an Amish parent who had been convicted of
violating Wisconsin's compulsory attendance laws.[10] Yoder had
refused to send his child to public schools beyond the eighth
grade despite a Wisconsin law that required attendance
through age sixteen.
    The test adopted by the Court in *Sherbert* and later refined
in *Yoder* consists of two parts that apply to the person or
organization asserting a free exercise claim and two parts that
apply to the government agency against which the claim is
asserted. In order to satisfy the test, a claimant must show (1)
that her conduct is motivated by sincere religious belief and
(2) that the state has imposed a substantial burden on that
conduct. It is important to note that a belief need not be
reasonable, logical, or acceptable to others; it need only be
sincere.[11]
    If the claimant satisfies these two criteria, she will prevail

unless the state can show that the restriction on religious practice (1) is in furtherance of a compelling governmental interest and (2) is the least restrictive means of achieving that interest. Thus, the claimant will prevail in spite of a state's compelling interest if a means of furthering that interest can be found that imposes a lesser burden on the claimant's religious practice.

Recent Supreme Court decisions have cast serious doubts on the viability of the *Sherbert* test. The Court has held that the test does not apply to free exercise claims raised within prisons[12] or the military.[13] More importantly, the Court in *Employment Division v. Smith* (1990) held that the test may not apply to burdens on religious exercise that result from facially neutral, generally applicable laws, which is the way most current Free Exercise Clause cases arise.[14]

In *Smith*, the Supreme Court upheld a denial of unemployment compensation benefits to two drug rehabilitation counselors who had been fired for ingesting peyote in Native American worship services. In denying their claim, the Court severely limited the application of the *Sherbert* test. Generally, the compelling interest test will apply only (1) where religion has been targeted or singled out for discriminatory treatment, as in the case of a law forbidding an activity only if it is religiously motivated, (2) where a free exercise claim is linked with another constitutional right such as freedom of speech, press, or association, or (3) where the restriction on religious exercise occurs in a context that lends itself to individualized government assessment of the reasons for the relevant conduct, such as the unemployment compensation field. In other words, if the government's otherwise universal rule makes exceptions for a variety of secular reasons (good cause, hardship, or the like), religious practice must also be accepted as an exception. The Supreme Court in *Smith* did reiterate that government may not compel affirmation of religious belief or impose special disabilities on the basis of religion. Where a specific religion is targed for regulation, the Free Exercise Clause will be violated unless the government can demonstrate a compelling interest.[15]

Federal legislation (*i.e.*, the Religious Freedom Restoration Act, 42 U.S.C. 2000bb) has been passed to restore the compelling interest test and to ensure its application in all cases where religious exercise is burdened (*see* chapter 16). And several states have refused to follow the *Smith* rationale, continuing to apply strict scrutiny to all free exercise claims under their own constitutions.[16]

What is meant by a "compelling" governmental interest?

A compelling interest has been described by the Court as one of the "highest order"[17] and involving "some substantial threat to public safety, peace and order."[18] In the words of the Court, "Only the gravest abuses, endangering paramount interests, give occasion for permissible limitation."[19]

Some have suggested that the Supreme Court's record on free exercise cases belies its lofty rhetorical commitments. For example, a compelling state interest in preserving the integrity of the Social Security fund was found in a case where only a handful of Amish employers sought an exemption.[20]

Must a person believe in God in order to be protected by the Free Exercise Clause?

No. The Court has recognized that many religions are non-theistic—that is, they do not profess belief in a supreme being.[21] At one time, the Court recognized that ethical precepts and practices that occupy a place parallel to traditional religious beliefs should be considered "religious" for legal purposes.[22] *Wisconsin v. Yoder* suggests that the Free Exercise Clause protects only theistic faiths.[23] Courts tend to take a functional, as opposed to creedal, approach to the concept of religion, protecting all beliefs and practices that occupy a place in the life of a claimant parallel to that of religion, including atheism, agnosticism, and secular humanism.[24] Of course, it is clear that no person may be compelled to accept any religion.[25] In any event, too strict a creedal approach risks the exclusion of some religions and could run afoul of the Establishment Clause prohibition against preferring one religion over another.[26]

Do religious persons have the right to spread their beliefs?

Yes. Religious speech is as protected as other forms of speech. People are free to communicate their religious views. They may not be silenced merely because some people would prefer not to hear their views. In particular, religious people may speak freely in places such as parks and on sidewalks and are free to deliver literature door to door. Of course, like all speech, religious speech may be subject to content-neutral time, place, or manner restrictions, *e.g.*, the government may prohibit all speakers from using loudspeakers after midnight in residential areas.[27]

NOTES

1. *See* n. 1, ch. 1.
2. *Cantwell v. Connecticut*, 310 U.S. 296 (1940).
3. *See Cantwell, supra.*
4. *See Swaggart v. Board of Equalization*, 493 U.S. 378 (1990).
5. *Reynolds v. United States*, 98 U.S. 145 (1878); *Cantwell, supra.*
6. *Jehovah's Witnesses v. King County Hospital*, 278 F. Supp. 488 (W.D. Wash. 1967), *aff'd. mem.*, 390 U.S. 598 (1968).
7. *Reynolds v. United States*, 98 U.S. (Otto) 145 (1878) (polygamy); *Prince v. Massachusetts*, 321 U.S. 158 (1944) (child labor).
8. *See Frazee v. Illinois Department of Employment Security*, 489 U.S. 829, 832–34 (1989).
9. 374 U.S. 398 (1963).
10. *Wisconsin v. Yoder*, 406 U.S. 205 (1972).
11. *United States v. Ballard*, 322 U.S. 78 (1944); *Thomas v. Review Board*, 450 U.S. 707 (1981).
12. *O'Lone v. Estate of Shabazz*, 482 U.S. 342 (1987).
13. *Goldman v. Weinberger*, 475 U.S. 503 (1986).
14. 494 U.S. 872 (1990).
15. *Church of the Lukumi Babalu Aye v. City of Hialeah*, 113 S. Ct. 2217 (1993).
16. *E.g.*, *Minnesota v. Hershberger*, 462 N.W.2d 393 (Minn. 1990); *Society of Jesus v. Boston Landmarks Commission*, 409 Mass. 38, 564 N.E.2d 571 (1990); *Rupert v. City of Portland*, 605 A.2d 63 (Me. 1992).
17. *Thomas, supra* at 718.
18. *Sherbert, supra* at 403.
19. *Sherbert, supra* at 406 (quoting *Thomas v. Collins*, 323 U.S. 516, 530 (1945)).
20. *See United States v. Lee*, 455 U.S. 252 (1982).
21. *Torcaso v. Watkins*, 367 U.S. 488 (1961).
22. *Gillette v. United States*, 401 U.S. 437 (1971).
23. 406 U.S. 205, 215–16 (1972).
24. *See also Malnak v. Yogi*, 592 F.2d 197 (1979); *Africa v. State of Pennsylvania*, 662 F.2d 1025, *cert. denied*, 456 U.S. 908 (1982).

25. *Wallace v. Jaffree*, 472 U.S. 38, 92–114 (Rehnquist, J., dissenting).
26. *See Larson v. Valente*, 456 U.S. 228 (1982).
27. *Lamb's Chapel v. Center Moriches School District*, 113 S. Ct. 2141 (1993); *Jamison v. Texas*, 318 U.S. 413 (1943); *Bacon v. Bradley-Bourbonaise High School Dist.*, 707 F. Supp. 1005 (C.D. Ill. 1989).

VIII

Accommodation of Religion

What is accommodation of religion?

Accommodation of religion is the practice of drafting government policy in a manner that allows persons to exercise their religion as freely as possible. Accommodation may consist of policies aimed specifically at religion, such as a program that releases students from public schools for religious instruction.[1] More often, it may involve the creation of exemptions or exceptions from laws of general application in order to avoid placing burdens on religious exercise. Professor Laurence Tribe has identified three categories of religious accommodation: required, permissible, and impermissible.[2]

When is accommodation required?

As noted in chapter 7, accommodation may be required when government has placed a substantial burden on religious exercise unless the government action (1) is justified by a compelling governmental interest and (2) is the least restrictive means of accomplishing that interest.

Examples of required religious accommodation include the excusal of Amish schoolchildren from compulsory attendance laws after the eighth grade,[3] the excusal of Sabbatarians from the requirement to accept Saturday work under a state's unemployment compensation plan,[4] the exemption of a church sanctuary from a landmarking ordinance that forbade certain renovation,[5] and the exemption from a state fair housing law of a couple who refused, on religious grounds, to rent to an unmarried couple when the state had placed similar disabilities on unmarried couples at state universities.[6]

There might be instances when the state's compelling interest in denying a request for accommodation is enforcement of the Establishment Clause. For example, a high school student's religion might require that she pray five times a day in a room designated solely for prayer. Notwithstanding her sincere religious belief, a public school probably could not set aside a room exclusively for prayer without violating the Establishment Clause.

What is permissible accommodation?
In some cases, accommodation for religion may not be required, yet be permissible. An example is found in Section 702 of the Civil Rights Act of 1964,[7] which permits religious organizations to discriminate on the basis of religion in employment even in cases where the employee performs no apparent religious duties. In *Presiding Bishop v. Amos*[8] a unanimous Supreme Court rejected an Establishment Clause challenge to this exemption and allowed a church-affiliated gymnasium to fire a custodian who was not in good standing with the church. The rationale for the decision was that Section 702 merely lifts a governmentally imposed burden that could have forced religious organizations to hire individuals who did not support the organization's religious mission. Of particular concern was the possibility that judges would be called upon to determine which employees performed religious functions and which did not.

Other examples of permissible accommodation include 42 U.S.C. § 2000e-2, which requires employers to accommodate the religious practices of employees, such as sabbath observance, if it can be done without "undue hardship," 50 App. U.S.C. § 456, which exempts conscientious objectors from the draft, and 26 U.S.C. §§ 6033 and 7611, which excuse churches from providing certain information to the Internal Revenue Service.

What is impermissible accommodation?
Accommodation is impermissible when it has the primary effect of advancing religion.

In *Estate of Thornton v. Caldor, Inc.*[9] the Court struck down a Connecticut law that forbade employers from refusing an employee's request to observe his sabbath despite possible hardship on the employer or other employees. Similarly, the Court struck down a Texas sales tax exemption provided exclusively for religious periodicals.[10] Such an exemption provided an indirect subsidy to religious speech and could not be justified as alleviating any significant burden on the free exercise of religion.

Does the Constitution require the government to accommodate religion by providing tax credits, vouchers, or other financial assistance for those who wish to attend or send their children to religious schools?

No. The courts have made clear that the First Amendment does not give persons the right to demand that government finance their religious choices. To the contrary, courts have generally struck down such assistance as violating the Establishment Clause.[11]

NOTES

1. *See Zorach v. Clauson*, 343 U.S. 306 (1952).
2. L. Tribe, *American Constitutional Law*, § 14-4 (1988).
3. *Wisconsin v. Yoder*, 406 U.S. 205 (1972).
4. *Sherbert v. Verner*, 374 U.S. 398 (1963); *Thomas v. Review Board*, 450 U.S. 707 (1981).
5. *Society of Jesus v. Boston Landmarks Commission*, 409 Mass. 38, 564 N.E.2d 571 (1990).
6. *Donahue v. Fair Employment and Housing Commission*, 2 Cal. Rptr. 2d 32 (Cal. App. 2 Dist. 1991).
7. 42 U.S.C. § 2000e-1.
8. 483 U.S. 327 (1987).
9. 472 U.S. 703 (1985).
10. *Texas Monthly v. Bullock*, 489 U.S. 1 (1989).
11. *Lemon v. Kurtzman*, 403 U.S. 602 (1971); *Committee for Public Education and Religious Liberty v. Nyquist*, 413 U.S. 756 (1973); *see also Witters v. Washington Department of Services for the Blind*, 474 U.S. 481 (1986); *Mozert v. Hawkins County Board of Education*, 765 F.2d 75 (1986).

IX

Church Autonomy: Claims
Against Religious Organizations
and Intrachurch Disputes

Can lawsuits be filed against churches and other religious organizations?

As a general rule, yes. While a few states have retained some semblance of charitable immunity,[1] most jurisdictions permit lawsuits to be filed against churches and other religious organizations.[2]

What about claims of so-called clergy malpractice?

Because the theory of clergy malpractice would require courts to establish a standard of care and conduct for a religious profession, the theory is almost certainly unconstitutional.[3] On the other hand, some complaints against clergy (such as those involving sexual misconduct) can be maintained under traditional tort theories such as assault, battery, breach of fiduciary duty, outrageous conduct, and infliction of emotional distress.[4]

Are there other claims against religious organizations that are beyond the jurisdictions of secular courts?

Yes. The Supreme Court has made clear that questions involving church doctrine, governance, polity, administration, and other ecclesiastical matters lie beyond the jurisdiction of secular courts.[5] For example, the Court in *Serbian Eastern Orthodox Diocese v. Milivojevich*[6] held that the dismissal of a clergyman was not reviewable by the courts even in the face of allegations of arbitrary and capricious action by the church hierarchy. Similarly, the Eleventh Circuit Court of Appeals in *Crowder v. Southern Baptist Convention*[7] refused to review alleged violations of *Robert's Rules of Order* that occurred during the election of ecclesiastical officers at the denomination's annual convention.

What about property disputes between factions within a church or religious organization?

As a general rule, courts treat such disputes as ecclesiastical questions and will decline jurisdiction.[8] Where the religious organization is hierarchical, courts will defer to the highest adjudicatory body of the organization.[9] With congregational religious bodies courts will defer to the will of the majority of the members of each congregation.[10] The Supreme Court has sanctioned an alternative approach to church property disputes if the matter can be resolved by the application of neutral principles of law and involves no determination of church doctrine and belief.[11] For example, a court may take jurisdiction over an intrachurch property dispute where the case can be resolved by examining deeds, corporate charters, and similar documents, and these may be applied without resolving religious questions.[12]

Are religious organizations subject to antidiscrimination and other labor laws?

Partially. As indicated, the relationship between a religious organization and its clergy lies beyond the reach of civil authorities.[13] For that reason, antidiscrimination claims generally cannot be maintained by clergy.

On the other hand, the First Amendment does not shield religious organizations from all claims related to employment. For example, the Fair Labor Standards Act may require churches to pay nonministerial employees the minimum wage.[14] Similarly, religious organizations may be subject to discrimination claims by nonministerial employees based upon race, gender, or national origin.[15] Whether a particular employee is treated as "ministerial" will depend on the functions that employee performs. If, for example, the employee (though not ordained) performs such ministerial functions as preaching, teaching, conducting weddings and funerals, administering sacraments and church ordinances, and leading worship, the employee may be deemed a minister for legal purposes.[16]

What about claims of defamation or violations of privacy that arise out of church disciplinary procedures?

Some churches discipline members who violate the teachings of the church. Discipline can include termination of membership, shunning, ostracism, and public disclosure of the individual's misconduct. Generally, churches have the right to determine their own internal matters, including issues of church discipline. By uniting with a church, a member gives implied consent to abide by its teachings and its disciplinary process.[17] Notwithstanding the church's right to set qualifications for membership, there are limits on the right to discipline individual members.

In *Guinn v. Church of Christ of Collinsville*,[18] the Supreme Court of Oklahoma made clear that the First Amendment protects not only the freedom to worship but also the freedom *not* to worship. Even if a church has no provision for the withdrawal of membership or if the church denies the withdrawal of membership, an individual is legally free to terminate his or her association with a religious organization. Thus, the plaintiff in *Guinn* was entitled to sue the church for violation of privacy where the elders publicized her misconduct after she had voluntarily withdrawn her membership.

Similarly, in *Gorman v. Swaggart*,[19] a Louisiana court of appeals held that a religious organization was not free to publicize facts about a minister's sexual improprieties *beyond* the membership of the church. Thus, a church's right to discipline its members is conditional and can be lost if the church acts maliciously or in bad faith. This conditional privilege has been interpreted broadly, however, to shield religious organizations from liability for acts that might otherwise give rise to a cause of action for outrageous conduct or emotional distress.[20]

Can a church publicly discipline a member, revealing in the process information received from the member in confidential communications?

Probably not. As a rule, communications made to clergy acting in their professional capacity and intended to be confidential cannot be revealed to third parties.[21]

Are there statutory protections for religious institutions that go beyond what is required by the First Amendment?

Yes. Congress and other legislative bodies often create exemptions for religious organizations from generally applicable laws. These exemptions may or may not be required by the First Amendment. For example, Congress in 1972 amended

Title VII[22] of the Civil Rights Act of 1964 to permit religious organizations to discriminate on the basis of religion in employment even for employees whose responsibilities appear to be exclusively secular in nature.

When a church-owned gymnasium fired one of its custodians for failure to contribute a certain percentage of his income to the church, the exemption was challenged as a violation of the Establishment Clause. The district court sustained the challenge but was reversed by a unanimous Supreme Court.[23] While the Court did not hold that the statutory exemption for religious organizations under Title VII was required by the Free Exercise Clause, Justice William Brennan came close to doing so in his concurring opinion. Quoting Professor Douglas Laycock of the University of Texas Law School, Brennan wrote: "[R]eligious organizations have an interest in autonomy in ordering their internal affairs, so that they may be free to 'select their own leaders, define their own doctrines, resolve their own disputes, and run their own institutions. Religion includes important communal elements for most believers. They exercise their religion through religious organizations, and these organizations must be protected by the [Free Exercise] clause.'"[24] *Id.* at 341.

NOTES

1. *E.g.*, Maryland.

2. *Wollersheim v. Church of Scientology of California*, 4 Cal. App. 4th 1047 (Cal. Ct. App. 1992); *Karen S. v. Streitferdt*, 172 A.P.2d 440, 568 N.Y.S.2d 946 (1st Dept., 1991); *St. Casimer Church v. Frankiewics*, 563 N.E.2d 1331 (Ind. App. 1990); *J. v. Victory Tabernacle Baptist Church*, 372 S.E.2d 391 (Va. 1988).

3. See *Nally v. Grace Community Church of the Valley*, 47 Cal. 3d 278, 253 Cal. Rptr. 97, 736 P.2d 948 (1988); *Handley v. Richards*, 518 So. 2d 682 (Ala. 1987); *Hester v. Barnette*, 723 S.W.2d 544 (Mo. 1987); *Doe v. Indian Hills Community Church*, No. 424-159, (Dist. Ct. Neb. 1988); see also Esbeck, *Tort Claims Against Churches and Ecclesiastical Officers: The First Amendment Considerations*, 89 W. Va. L. Rev. 1 (1986); Comment, *Made Out of Whole Cloth? A Constitutional Analysis of the Clergy Malpractice Concept*, 19 Cal. W. L. Rev. 507 (1983); Ericsson, *Clergy Malpractice: Ramifications of a New Theory*, 16 Val. U. L. Rev. 163 (1981).

4. *See Byrd v. Faber,* 565 N.E.2d 584 (Ohio 1991); *Ericsson v. Chris-tenson,* 99 Or. App. 104, 781 P.2d 383 (1989); *Destafano v. Grabrian,* 729 P.2d 1018 (Colo. 1986).

5. *Watson v. Jones,* 80 U.S. (13 Wall.) 679 (1872); *Gonzalez v. Roman Catholic Archbishop of Manila,* 280 U.S. 1 (1929). *See also* Laycock, *Towards a General Theory of the Religion Clauses: The Case of Church Labor Relations and the Right to Church Autonomy,* 81 Colum. L. Rev. 1373 (1981); Esbeck, *Establishment Clause Limits on Governmental Interference with Religious Organizations,* 41 Wash. & Lee L. Rev. 347 (1984).

6. 426 U.S. 696 (1976).

7. 828 F.2d 718 (11th Cir. 1987), *cert. denied,* 484 U.S. 1066 (1988).

8. *E.g., Watson v. Jones, supra.*

9. *E.g., Presbyterian Church v. Mary Elizabeth Blue Hull Memorial Presbyterian Church,* 393 U.S. 440 (1969); *Kedroff v. Saint Nicholas Cathedral,* 344 U.S. 94 (1952).

10. *See Crowder v. Southern Baptist Convention, supra.*

11. *Jones v. Wolf,* 443 U.S. 595 (1979).

12. *Fry v. Emmanuel Churches of Christ,* Inc., 839 S.W.2d 406 (Tenn. App. 1992).

13. *See Serbian Eastern Orthodox Diocese v. Milivojevich, supra; McClure v. Salvation Army,* 460 F.2d 553 (5th Cir. 1972) (holding that an officer in the Salvation Army was not protected by Title VII despite the fact that most of her duties were clerical); *Rayburn v. General Conference of Seventh-day Adventists,* 772 F.2d 1164 (4th Cir. 1985); *Hutchinson v. Thomas,* 789 F.2d 392 (6th Cir. 1986), *cert. denied,* 479 U.S. 885 (1986); *see also O'Connor Hospital v. Superior Court,* 195 C.A.3d 546, 240 Cal. Rptr. 766 (1987) (hospital chaplains); *Maguire v. Marquette University,* 627 F. Supp. 1499 (E.D. Wis. 1986), *modified,* 814 F.2d 1213 (7th Cir. 1987) (religion professor); *Pime v. Loyola University of Chicago,* 803 F.2d 351 (1986) (religion professor).

14. *Tony and Susan Alamo Foundation v. Secretary of Labor,* 471 U.S. 290 (1985); *E.E.O.C. v. Tree of Life Christian School,* 751 F. Supp. 700 (S.D. Ohio 1991).

15. *E.E.O.C. v. Pacific Press Publishing Association,* 676 F.2d 1272 (9th Cir. 1982) (editorial secretary at church-affiliated publishing house); *E.E.O.C. v. Mississippi College,* 626 F.2d 477 (5th Cir. 1980) (psychology teacher at Baptist college); *Russell v. Belmont College,* 554 F. Supp. 667 (N.D. Tenn. 1982) (education professor at Baptist college); *but see Madsen v. Erwin,* 481 N.E.2d 1160 (Mass. 1985); *E.E.O.C. v. Fremont Christian School,* 781 F.2d 1362 (9th Cir. 1986); *E.E.O.C. v. Southwestern Baptist Theological Seminary,* 651 F.2d 277 (5th Cir. 1981), *cert. denied,* 456 U.S. 905 (1982).

16. *Southwestern Baptist Theological Seminary, supra; McClure v. Salvation Army, supra.* One commentator has stated: "As a general rule, if the employee's primary duties consist of teaching, spreading the faith, church governance, the supervision of a religious order, or supervision of or participation in religious ritual and worship, he or she would be considered 'clergy.'" Bagni, *Discrimination in the Name of the Lord: A Critical Evaluation of Discrimination by Religious Organizations*, 79 Colum. L. Rev. 1514 (1979).

    For a lengthy analysis of the application of antidiscrimination laws to religious institutions *see* Thomas, *The Application of AntiDiscrimination Laws to Religious Institutions: The Irresistible Force Meets the Immoveable Object*, 12 J. Nat'l. A. Admin. L. Judges 83 (1992).

17. *See* L. Buzzard and T. Brandon, Jr., *Church Discipline and the Courts* (1987).

18. 775 P.2d 766 (Okla. 1989).

19. 524 So. 2d 915 (1988).

20. *See Paul v. Watchtower Bible and Tract Society*, 819 F.2d 875 (9th Cir. 1987). This case was decided prior to *Employment Division v. Smith*, 494 U.S. 872 (1990) and might be decided differently today under the Free Exercise Clause. Most likely, the case would be treated as a hybrid association/free exercise claim, yielding the same result. So would the Religious Freedom Restoration Act, 42 U.S.C. § 2000bb.

21. *See* ch. 13.

22. *See* 42 U.S.C. § 2000e-1.

23. *Corporation of the Presiding Bishop v. Amos*, 483 U.S. 327 (1987).

24. *Id.* at 341.

X

Conscientious Objection

Are individuals who have religious objections to participating in war entitled to avoid the military draft or actual military service?

The Supreme Court has never recognized such a right under the Free Exercise Clause of the First Amendment. Generally, all it has done is interpret what Congress did in creating exemptions in the Military Selective Service Act for "conscientious objectors." At the present time, federal law recognizes two kinds of conscientious objectors: (1) persons who "by reason of religious training and belief" are "conscientiously opposed to participation in war in any form" and (2) persons who by reason of similar beliefs and training are opposed to combatant service, but who do not object to performing noncombatant services, such as medical care.[1] Individuals who believe they fit within those definitions, however, must still register with the Selective Service System when they become eighteen years of age.

Does a person seeking status as a conscientious objector need to believe in a Supreme Being?

At one time Congress had placed such a limitation in the Military Selective Service Act. The Supreme Court rejected a narrow reading of this language that required a belief in God, noting that the proper test is "whether a given belief that is sincere and meaningful occupies a place in the life of its possessor parallel to that filled by the orthodox belief in God."[2] Although the Court has acknowledged that Congress had the authority in the Act not to include "essentially political, sociological, or philosophical views, or a merely personal moral code" as adequate "religious training and belief," it also concluded that conscientious objector status could not be denied simply because an otherwise qualified person also had strong political beliefs about matters of public policy such as war.[3]

Must a person seeking conscientious objector status oppose all war?

Although many religious groups draw detailed distinctions between "just" and "unjust" wars, the Supreme Court has not required that Congress include "selective" conscientious objectors as a category for exemption from military service.[4] It is permissible, therefore, for Congress to require that a conscientious objector oppose all wars, or war in any form, and not merely have an opposition to a particular war. In doing so, the Court specifically rejected the argument that denial of such status to persons who believed in selective objection violated the Establishment Clause by granting preference to those traditionally religious groups (such as Quakers and Mennonites, for example) who oppose participation in all wars.

May courts question the sincerity of persons claiming conscientious objector status?

Yes. The Supreme Court has permitted inquiry into the sincerity of an individual's claim, but requires a "basis in fact" for denial of such a claim.[5]

Determining a "basis in fact" is not easy, but requires a statement of reasons, not mere suspicious or subjective opinions. Summarizing the law, one court has articulated that: "[a] basis in fact will not find support in mere disbelief or surmise as to the applicant's motivation. Rather, the government must show some hard, reliable, provable facts which would provide a basis for disbelieving the applicant's sincerity, or it must show something concrete in the record which substantially blurs the picture painted by the applicant."[6]

Are conscientious objectors entitled to educational benefits under the GI Bill?

No. The Supreme Court has ruled that persons who perform "alternate civilian service" need not be covered by the Veterans' Readjustment Benefits Act. It reasoned that denial of educational benefits was only an "incidental" burden on the free exercise of religion and that the level of disruptions caused by military service and alternative service are sufficiently different that Congress could rationally deny benefits to the latter.[7]

Once an individual is in the military, can he or she be discharged as a conscientious objector?

Yes, discharge as a conscientious objector is permitted under regulations issued by the Department of Defense, but only if an applicant can show a change or strengthening of his or her beliefs since enlistment.[8] A person who is unsuccessful in obtaining an administrative discharge from the service can also seek relief through the federal courts. The standards for exemption under the Selective Service Act are also applicable to in-service claims.[9]

NOTES

1. 50 U.S.C. App. § 450.
2. *Seeger v. United States*, 380 U.S. 163 (1965).
3. *Welsh v. United States*, 398 U.S. 333 (1970).
4. *Gillette v. United States*, 401 U.S. 437 (1971).
5. *Witmer v. United States*, 348 U.S. 375 (1954).
6. *Smith v. Laird*, 486 F.2d 307, 310 (10th Cir. 1973).
7. *Johnson v. Robison*, 415 U.S. 361 (1974).
8. DoD Directive 1300. 6.
9. *See, e.g., Hager v. Sec. of Air Force*, 938 F.2d 1449 (1st Cir. 1991).

XI

Refusal of Medical Treatment on Religious Grounds

Can a competent adult refuse medical treatment, even if there is a reasonable certainty it will save his or her life?

In general, competent adults can refuse treatment on any grounds whatsoever. Numerous state courts have concluded that a generally articulated state intent in the "preservation of life" is not sufficient to override a patient's right to decide for himself or herself what procedures, if any, to undertake.[1]

One would assume that a religious basis for the refusal would enhance the likelihood that a patient's refusal of medical treatment would be respected. This is not always the case, however. When physicians see an individual who is in need of what they perceive as relatively minor medical intervention (such as a blood transfusion) and they are relatively unfamiliar with the religious beliefs being asserted (for example, those of Jehovah's Witnesses), they may consider those persons even irrational, perhaps even legally incompetent. They sometimes then provide the undesired treatment.

Courts remain divided over whether physicians may substitute their judgment for those of patients under these circumstances. Some have ruled that a general state interest in the "preservation of life" will warrant coerced transfusions,[2] but a larger number reject the sufficiency of such an interest. One court observed that such a standard was "quite antithetical to our fundamental thesis that the role of the state is to ensure a maximum of individual freedom of choice and conduct."[3]

Where death resulting from the refusal of a transfusion would leave unattended minor children, the judicial calculus tends to shift. Courts are more likely to order treatments such as transfusions where the death of a patient would lead to children becoming orphaned and wards of the state, a kind of "one parent is enough" rule.[4]

In one case, a federal court justified court-ordered transfusion on the theory that since the act is compelled, rather than voluntary, the patient's conscience would be clear and he or she would suffer no spiritual retribution.[5] (This "theological" theory is now generally rejected by Jehovah's Witnesses adherents.)

Under circumstances where the transfusion is not justified by whatever standard the jurisdiction has adopted, a transfused patient may be able to sue the parties responsible for the undesired treatment, particularly if there is a clear and contemporaneous declaration by a patient for nontreatment or a specific promise from hospital authorities that a transfusion will not occur.[6] A federal civil rights claim may even be permitted under appropriate circumstances.[7]

Can an adult refuse such treatment for a child under his or her legal authority?

In these cases, courts generally reject a parent's authority to avoid life-sustaining treatments. Most courts concur that parents have a legal obligation to provide "necessary medical care," and where rejection of care is not in the "best interests of the child" the state may require treatment. In these cases, a court often appoints a person (on the staff of the hospital in which the child may be, for example) to serve as guardian and make decisions in the child's best interest.[8]

Although one case holds that even treatment (which included a blood transfusion) for a non-life-threatening condition can be performed over religious objection,[9] most decisions do not support state interference under these circumstances.[10]

Can parents refuse vaccination for their children on religious grounds?

There is no established constitutional right to refuse vaccination.[11] However, many states will permit persons with religious objection to immunization programs to forgo them. It is probably true that all sincerely held religious objections, whether as a part of an established theological doctrine such as Christian Science or as an individually articulated belief, must be accorded the same deference in such a system.[12] These states also generally will require vaccination when health authorities declare an epidemic to exist, thus heightening the danger that nonvaccinated persons will be transmitters of the disease.

May parents be held criminally liable for failing to provide medical treatment for ill children based on their religious convictions?

There have been several successful prosecutions under state criminal law of parents who provide prayer-based treatment or other spiritual approaches in lieu of traditional medical care. This is an area of law complicated by the more than forty state law provisions that specifically exempt parents who provide spiritual rather than medical treatment for ill children from being charged under civil child neglect or child endangerment laws.

In several jurisdictions, parents who relied on these exemptions have successfully defended themselves on the basis of these exemptions in subsequent criminal prosecutions. In Minnesota, for example, indictments against two Christian Science parents for felony child endangerment and involuntary manslaughter were dismissed when the court found they had reasonably relied on the state's child neglect exemption. The court refused to force these parents to assume that if the spiritual treatments failed, they would face other criminal charges.[13] Similarly, a Florida court overturned parents' convictions for criminal child abuse where use of spiritual methods by a Christian Science practitioner failed to save the life of their seven-year-old daughter, who had a diabetic condition. The trial court had allowed the jury to determine the "reasonableness" of the use of this alternative technique, even where "the actions are based on sincerely held beliefs." Apparently, the jury judged reasonableness based on the conduct of the general public and found the parents' Christian Science beliefs unreasonable. On appeal, the reviewing court found that the child neglect statute exemption upon which the parents relied did not give proper notice that the state might prosecute if the decision to forgo traditional medical treatments proved unsuccessful.[14]

On the other hand, some states have narrowed the basis for such a defense or rejected it completely. Colorado has held that a statutory affirmative defense to a child prosecution of "treatment by spiritual means" is available only where a parent, in good faith, holds an "objectively reasonable belief" that the child is not in a life-threatening condition or in a condition with substantial risk of serious bodily harm.[15] In one highly publicized California case, a mother was convicted of involuntary manslaughter and child endangerment after the death of her daughter from meningitis, which had been treated exclusively through prayer.[16] The Court seemed to conclude that it was not "sinful" for a Christian Scientist to utilize medical intervention and that the belief in spiritual healing was not "central" to the faith (both arguably inaccurate and irrelevant as a legal matter), which led it to question whether any significant burden on religious faith was even involved in the case. In light of this view, it was clear to the court that "imposition of criminal liability for endangering or killing an ill child by failing to provide medical care furthers an interest of unparalleled significance: the protection of the very lives of California's children."[17] California courts thus have clearly adopted the view that sincerely held beliefs about the effectiveness of spiritual healing is no defense in a criminal case and that exemption in child neglect statutes does not bar prosecution for felony child endangerment.[18]

NOTES

1. *See generally*, G. Annas, *The Rights of Patients* (Carbondale: Southern Illinois University Press, 1989).
2. *See, e.g., John F. Kennedy Memorial Hosp. v. Heston*, 58 N.J. 576, 279 A.2d 670 (1971).
3. *In re Osborne*, 294 A.2d 372 (D.C.C.A. 1972), n. 13.
4. *Norwood Hospital v. Munoz*, 409 Mass. 116, 564 N.E. 2d 1017 (Mass. 1991) (no evidence that abandonment of child would occur in this two-parent family); *Fosmire v. Nicoleau 75 N.Y.2d 218*, 551 N.Y.S.2d 876, 551 N.E.2d 77 (1990) (parent's right to refuse not precluded, at least where another parent is available). Compare *In re Debrevil*, 603 So. 2d 538 (Fla. App. 4th Dist. 1992) (four children would become wards of the state). *See also Raleigh Fitkin-Paul Morgan Memorial Hospital v. Anderson*, 42 N.J. 421, 201 A.2d 537 (1964), *cert. denied*, 377 U.S. 985 (1964) (ordering blood transfusion for pregnant woman).
5. *United States v. George*, 239 F. Supp. 752 (D. Conn. 1965).
6. *Lunsford v. Regents of Univ. of Calif.*, (Sup. Ct. Cal. 1990) (breach of fiduciary duty, infliction of emotional distress, and violation of civil rights where parents had shown that the child's injury did not require a transfusion); *Werth v. Taylor*, 190 Mich. App. 141, 475 N.W. 2d 426 (1991), 11 RFR 226 (battery action would not lie where patient had

signed preadmission refusal of transfusion, but no contemporaneous refusal because she was unconscious).

7. *Holmes v. Silver Cross Hospital*, 340 F. Supp. 125 (N.D. Ill. 1972).

8. *State v. Perricane*, 34 N.J. 463, 181 A.2d. 751 (1962).

9. *In re Sampson*, 65 Misc.2d. 658, 317 N.Y.S.2d. 641 (1970), *aff'd*, 29 N.Y.2d. 900, 278 N.E.2d. 918 (1972) (severe facial deformity).

10. *In re Seiferth*, 309 N.Y. 80, 127 N.E.2d. 820 (1955) (repair of cleft palate).

11. *Jacobson v. Massachusetts*, 197 U.S. 11 (1904).

12. *Kolbeck v. Kramer*, 84 N.J. Super. 569, 202 A.2d. 889 (1964).

13. *Minnesota v. McKown*, 475 N.W.2d 63 (Minn. 1981).

14. *Hermanson v. Florida*, 604 So. 2d 775 (Fla. 1992).

15. *Lybarger v. Colorado*, 807 P.2d 570 (Colo. 1991).

16. *Walker v. Supreme Court*, 763 P.2d 852 (Cal. 1988), *cert. denied*, 491 U.S. 905 (1989). *See also Commonwealth v. Barnhart*, 345 Pa. Super. 10, 497 A.2d 616 (1985), *cert. denied*, 488 U.S. 817 (1988).

17. *Id.* at 869.

18. *People v. Rippberger*, 231 Cal. App. 3d 1667 (Cal. Ct. App. 1991).

XII

Zoning and Religious Institutions

In an environmentally sensitive age, it is no surprise that decisions about the uses of land have come under increased scrutiny. Religious institutions are now no exception.

As a matter of fact, religious institutions for a long time have not been subject to the same level of scrutiny that other users of land have been. There were two reasons for this favorable treatment: (1) the special constitutional protection afforded religious practice and (2) the uniquely favorable social status of religion. Both of these have eroded. With that erosion has come a noticeable and related decline in the protection offered religious institutions in land use regulation matters. These changes are not uniform, and the law in this area is far from settled. Still, it is now harder for religious institutions to gain permission to locate at a particular site than it used to be. Because in many places there is no undeveloped land available at reasonable prices, the rules take on increasing importance for religious institutions.

Are religious institutions immune from zoning laws?

Zoning laws have two components: one is procedural, requiring that potential users of land file an application with the appropriate authorities (*i.e.*, a planning board or a zoning board); the other is substantive, that is, that only certain uses of particular parcels of land are acceptable. This last class of rules is not always absolute; sometimes the rules can be waived or their requirements varied (these are called *variances*).

Claims for exemption from the procedural requirements of the zoning laws are rarely made by churches and almost never accepted;[¹] substantive decisions are frequently challenged successfully.

May zoning law or decision-making be used to exclude religious groups that are disliked or disfavored?

Whatever the validity of zoning laws as applied to religious institutions generally, it is clear that they may not be used to exclude religious institutions because the zoning authorities do not like the religion practiced in a particular temple, synagogue, mosque or church. Thus, where town officials routinely waived parking requirements for churches but refused to do so for a mosque, a federal court ordered the city to allow the mosque to function without regard to those requirements.[2]

Similarly, if a zoning decision is tainted by a desire to exclude a religious institution from a community because it would draw "undesirables" to the community (*e.g.*, Evangelicals, Orthodox Jews, Muslims, cults) it will not be allowed to stand. Not only would both of the federal Constitution's religion clauses be violated by such zoning; the zoning would probably violate the federal Fair Housing Act as well because its purpose would be to exclude a group of persons from residing in the community on the basis of religion.[3]

Does the federal Constitution itself require that religious institutions be given preferential treatment under zoning laws?

Because zoning laws can substantially impede the ability of groups of people to gather to worship God as they believe they are obligated to do, one would have thought that the United States Supreme Court would have held that zoning laws that impede the ability of churches to function would deny those institutions—and their adherents—the free exercise of religion and thus would have subjected these laws to strict scrutiny. However, long before the Court eviscerated the Free Exercise Clause in the *Smith*[4] case, the Court summarily held that forcing churches to comply with zoning laws in the same manner as other users of land did not violate the Constitution. The Court reasoned that zoning laws imposed only an indirect burden on religious practice.[5]

Generally speaking, the lower federal courts have continued to refuse to intervene in church zoning disputes, unless it is shown that the decision stems from a discriminatory motive.[6] Surprisingly however, after the *Smith* decision, which generally lessened the constitutional protections available to religious practice, one federal court of appeals held that religious institutions could raise free exercise claims to zoning ordinances on the theory that such cases were a hybrid between the Free Exercise and Free Speech Clauses and that applications of zoning laws to churches were subject to the compelling interest test. Zoning may thus be one of the few areas where *Smith* advanced the protection afforded by the Constitution's Free Exercise Clause.[7]

State courts have divided on this issue. Some courts, led by California,[8] have held that there is no constitutional impediment to applying zoning laws to religious institutions in the same way that they are applied to bakeries, apartment houses, and shopping centers. Under this rule, churches may be excluded entirely from residential areas.

Until recently, a majority of states, led by New York,[9] held that the zoning laws could not be so applied and that zoning power could not be used to deny a religious institution the right to build in a community or in residential zones. The New York courts reasoned that the zoning laws, which intrude on the rights of property owners, are valid only if they advance the public interest and that the public interest is advanced by permitting religious institutions to flourish.

More recently, however, the New York Court of Appeals has moved to a more moderate position. Religious institutions in New York no longer have an unfettered right to locate where they please. A municipality or other governmental unit may insist that a potential religious user apply for a special use permit. There is a mild presumption in favor of granting the application. If the presence of the institution on a particular plot of land will cause substantial harm to the community (*e.g.*, increased traffic and demand for parking, destruction of wetlands, changing patterns of water run-off, and the like), the municipality may impose restrictions on the property or the use of a particular religious institution to ameliorate these harms. Thus, for example, the municipality may require a certain number of parking spaces. In some instances, churches have been required to limit the number of persons attending services or limit the hours during which the church will hold services. Courts have tolerated these restrictions if they are related to the harm created by the use of the property.[10] Only if it is impossible to minimize the harm—and the harm is serious—may the municipality refuse to permit the institution to locate on the requested site.

New Jersey follows a third course.[11] It permits the ordinary zoning rules to be applied to religious institutions but is more lenient in granting churches variances from the usual requirements. For example, New Jersey ordinarily requires an applicant for a variance to show that its presence in the community will benefit the public and that the proposed use will not impose an undue burden on the community. Religious institutions are presumed to satisfy the first request and are to be judged leniently on the second.

Massachusetts has an unusual rule. It forbids the use of zoning laws to deny a religious institution the right to build on a particular site. Localities can regulate the size and bulk of a structure but only for legitimate zoning reasons, not as a subterfuge for excluding the institution from the site.[12]

Can a municipality decide to grant churches more favorable treatment?

In *Employment Division v. Smith*[13] the Court held that, while the federal Constitution did not require special treatment of religion, it tolerated a fair amount of it. Thus, it would appear that a municipality could exempt churches from parking and other restrictions applicable to other land users.

However, a California court has held that, under California's constitution, special treatment is permissible only to the extent that the Free Exercise Clause of the California or United States Constitution requires it. This confines zoning authorities to a fairly narrow band of accommodation of churches in the zoning context.[14]

What sort of restrictions have the courts upheld applied to churches?

Generally speaking, traffic restrictions (such as minimum number of parking spaces or the route by which vehicles exit the property), the location of a building on the site and lay-out restrictions designed to deal with the impact on surrounding properties, and other pure environmental decisions have been upheld.[15] States differ as to whether these rules are valid whatever their impact on churches or whether zoning authorities must prove that the harm exists in a particular case.[16] Thus, several courts have held that requirements for parking spaces cannot be enforced against Orthodox Jewish synagogues, to which worshippers do not drive to synagogue on sabbaths and holidays, because they serve no useful function.[17]

May a municipality wholly exclude churches from its boundaries?

The answer to this question is unclear. The general rule appears to be that notwithstanding the power of a municipality to control where a church is located within its boundaries, it may not wholly exclude them from its jurisdiction.[18]

Are there special rules for small, house churches?

Most zoning rules that apply to churches simply specify churches, whether they are designed for twenty people or two thousand. Thus, in these jurisdictions, a small congregation meeting in a person's home will be subject to all the ordinary zoning rules, which are typically irrelevant to the small congregation. Other jurisdictions apply somewhat more flexible rules to so-called house churches. They reason in part that these congregations do not impose a greater burden on a neighborhood than would a party given in a private house.[19]

May a church be given landmark status over its objections?

The courts that have addressed this question have divided. Some courts have rebuffed challenges to the involuntary landmarking of churches, on the ground that landmarking advances an important public interest and does not prevent churches from carrying out their religious mission but merely denies them the optimum return on their property.[20] At least one court has rejected landmarking of church buildings on the theory that it gives the government too much power over churches.[21]

These cases have generally involved only the landmarking of the outside of a church building, not the sanctuary. Many landmarking statutes prohibit the involuntary landmarking of church interiors. In the one instance in which a landmark commission attempted to landmark the interior of a church— to the point of telling the church where its altars could be located—its efforts were roundly rebuffed by the state's supreme court.[22]

NOTES

1. *See, e.g.*, *Grace Community Church v. Town of Bethel*, 30 Conn. App. 765, 622 A.2d 591 (1993).

2. *Marks v. City of Chesapeake*, 883 F.2d 304 (4th Cir. 1989); *Islamic Center v. City of Starkville*, 840 F.2d 293 (5th Cir. 1988).
3. *LeBlanc-Sternberg v. Fletcher*, 781 F. Supp. 261 (S.D.N.Y. 1991).
4. *See* ch. 7, *supra.*
5. *State ex rel Wisconsin Lutheran Conference v. Sinai*, 267 Wis. 91, 65 N.W.2d 43, *app. dismissed*, 349 U.S. 913 (1955); *Allendale Congregation v. Grosman*, 30 N.J. 273, 152 A.2d 569 (1959), *app. dismissed*, 361 U.S. 536 (1960); *Damascus Community Church v. Clackamas County*, 610 P.2d 273 (Or. App. 1980), *app. dismissed.* 450 U.S. 901 (1981).
6. *See, e.g., Christian Gospel Church v. City and County of San Francisco*, 896 F.2d 1224 (9th Cir. 1990); *Grosz v. City of Miami Beach*, 721 F.2d 729 (11th Cir. 1989); *Lubavitch Organization v. City of Lakewood*, 699 F.2d 303 (6th Cir. 1983).
7. *Cornerstone Bible Church v. City of Hastings*, 948 F.2d 464 (8th Cir. 1992).
8. *Corporation of the Presiding Bishop v. City of Porterville*, 203 P.2d 823, *aff'd*, 338 U.S. 805 (1949).
9. *Matter of Diocese of Rochester*, 1 N.Y.2d 508, 154 N.Y.S.2d 849, 136 N.E.2d 827 (1957).
10. *Cornell University v. Bagnardi*, 68 N.Y.2d 861, 510 N.Y.S.2d 861, 503 N.E.2d 509 (1986).
11. *E.g., Province of Meribah Society of Mary v. Village of Muttentown*, 148 A.D.2d 512, 538 N.Y.S.2d 850 (1989).
12. G.L. 40a, § 3. *Cf. Bible Speaks v. Board of Appeals of Lenox*, 8 Mass. App. 19, 391 N.E.2d 279 (1979); *Sisters of Holy Cross v. Town of Brookline*, 347 Mass. 486, 198 N.E.2d 625 (1964).
13. 494 U.S. 872 (1990), discussed in ch. 7, *supra.*
14. *Lucas Valley Homeowners Ass'n v. Marin County*, 233 Cal. App. 3d 130, 284 Cal. Rptr. 427 (1991).
15. *See* Anderson, *American Law of Zoning* (3d ed.) § 12.21, *et. seq.*
16. *Compare, North Syracuse First Baptist Church v. Village of North Syracuse*, 136 A.2d 942, 524 N.Y.S.2d 894 (4th Dept. 1933) with *Corporation of the Presiding Bishop of Porterville, supra*, note 8.
17. *E.g., Harrison Orthodox Minyan v. Town of Harrison*, 159 A.D.2d 572, 552 N.Y.S.2d 434 (2d Dept. 1990); *Orthodox Minyan of Elkins Park v. Chiltonham Twshp.*, 522 A.2d 772 (Commonwealth Court 1989).
18. *Cf. Borough of Mt. Ephraim v. Schaad*, 452 U.S. 61 (1981) (Justices differ on related question). *See Seward Chapel v. City of Seward*, 655 P.2d 1293, 1299 (Alaska 1992) (suggesting churches may not be zoned out of a city).
19. *See generally State v. Cameron*, 100 N.J. 586, 498 A.2d 1217 (1985).

20. *Ethical Culture Society v. Spatt*, 51 N.Y.2d 449, 434 N.Y. Supp. 2d 932, 415 N.E.2d 922 (1980); *Rector, Warden and Members v. City of New York*, 914 F.2d 348 (2d Cir. 1990).
21. *First Covenant Church of Seattle v. City of Seattle*, 120 Wash. 2d 203, 840 P.2d 174 (1992).
22. *Society of Jesus v. Boston Landmarks Comm'n*, 409 Mass. 38, 564 N.E.2d 571 (1970).

XIII
Clergy Confidentiality

Is the confidentiality of conversations between clergy and their counselees protected by law?

Yes. Virtually every state now has a statute that protects the confidentiality of communications between clergy and their counselees, and even federal common law recognizes the so-called priest-penitent privilege.[1]

How does one determine whether a particular communication is confidential?

To protect the confidentiality of communications, most states require (1) that the statement was made to a minister or at least to one who was reasonably assumed to be a minister,[2] (2) that the minister was acting in his or her professional capacity,[3] and (3) that there was a reasonable expectation of privacy. In short, the communication must be intended as confidential. Whether a particular communication is confidential may depend upon the policies and practices of the particular church or denomination.[4] A few states also require that the communication be penitential or confessional in nature.[5] The constitutionality of limiting confidentiality to this very narrow category of communication is questionable as it would appear to favor some religions over others.[6] For example, many evangelical churches do not encourage confession to a priest or minister but rather to God alone. Notwithstanding, such churches encourage their members to seek spiritual counsel from their clergy and almost universally consider such counseling to be confidential.

Who holds the privilege?

In most states the privilege is held by the person consulting the clergyman, but a few states such as New Jersey, Maryland, and Virginia allow the minister to claim or ignore the privilege without the person's consent.

Can the privilege be lost?

Yes. The most common reason for a counselee's losing the protection of the priest-penitent privilege is the presence of third parties. One court, for example, has held that a communication is not privileged if the minister's spouse is present. [7]

What about child abuse statutes that would force ministers to provide confidential information to the police?

All states now have some child abuse reporting law. Some exempt clergy; others do not. [8] The constitutionality of statutes that purport to override the priest-penitent privilege is debatable. There is little doubt that the state's interest in stopping child abuse is compelling, but forcing ministers to break their pledge of confidentiality would not appear to be the least restrictive means of doing so. [9] For example, a state could pursue its interest—as it pursues other criminal matters—through police investigations, informants and complaints. If the state is able to combat rape and homicide without forcing clergy to violate their religiously based obligations of confidentiality, why not child abuse?

Do clergy have a duty to warn third parties of imminent harm if they learn of this potential harm in a privileged communication?

Maybe. The California Supreme Court has suggested that clergy may have a duty to warn if there is a substantial likelihood of imminent bodily harm to third parties. [10] But a recent Louisiana decision suggests that clergy are under no obligation to warn third parties of potential harm. [11] Efforts to extend the duty to warn to the families of suicidal counselees have been unsuccessful. [12]

May counselees file suit against clergy where a breach of confidentiality has occurred?

In some states, yes. An increasing number of courts are recognizing a claim for invasion of privacy or breach of fiduciary duty where confidential communications have been revealed by clergy to third parties. These courts have ruled that holding clergy liable for such misconduct does not violate the First Amendment. [13]

NOTES

1. *In re Grand Jury Investigation*, 978 F.2d 374 (3d Cir. 1990). On the question of clergy confidentiality generally, *see* W. Tiemann and J. Bush, *The Right to Silence* (1983).
2. *Buttecali v. United States*, 130 F.2d 172 (5th Cir. 1942); *In re Murtha*, 115 N.J. Super. 380, 279 A.2d 889 (1971), *cert. denied*, 59 N.J. 239, 281 A.2d 278 (1971); *Eckmann v. Board of Education*, 106 F.R.D. 70 (1985); *In re Verplank*, 329 F. Supp. 433 (1971).
3. *Magar v. State of Arkansas*, 308 Ark. 380 (Ark. 1992); *State v. Boling*, 806 S.W.2d 202 (Tenn. App. 1990); *People v. Reyes*, 545 N.Y.S.2d 653 (1989).
4. *People v. Edwards*, 203 Cal. App. 3d 1358 (1988).
5. Arizona, California, Idaho, Indiana, Michigan, Montana, Nevada, Utah, Washington, and Wyoming.
6. *Scott v. Hammock*, 1990 W.L. 199912 (C.D. Utah 1990).
7. *State v. Melvin*, 564 A.2d 458 (N.H. 1989).
8. *State v. Motherwell*, 768 P.2d 1066 (Wash. 1990).
9. *Scott v. Hammock*, *supra* note 6; *see also Sherbert v. Verner*, 374 U.S. 398 (1963), *Wisconsin v. Yoder*, 406 U.S. 205 (1972).
10. *Tarasoff v. Regents*, 551 P.2d 334 (Cal. 1976).
11. *Miller v. Everett*, 576 So. 2d 1162 (La. App. 1991).
12. *Nally v. Grace Community Church*, 47 Cal. 3d 278, 253 Cal. Rptr. 97, 736 P.2d 948 (1988); *Bellah v. Greeson*, 81 Cal. App. 3d 614, 164 Cal. Rptr. 535 (1978).
13. *E.g.*, *Snyder v. Evangelical Orthodox Church*, 264 Cal. Rptr. 640 (Cal. App. 1989).

XIV

Religion in the Workplace

Does the Constitution require an employer to accommodate an employee's religious practice?

The Constitution applies only to government activities, not purely private activities. It thus provides no protection for employees of nongovernment employers and only uncertain protection for government employees. However, Title VII of the 1964 Civil Rights Act[1] provides that an employer (a term that includes unions) may not discriminate against a person because he adheres to a particular faith or none (*i.e.*, Baptists, Jews, or atheists), and that employers must accommodate an employee's religious practices unless doing so would cause undue hardship to the employer.[2] The Supreme Court has held that anything more than a *de minimis* burden on employers is not required by the statute.[3] An employee does not have any right to demand the most favorable possible accommodation.[4] Still, the Act has required accommodation of a wide variety of employee religious practices, including time off for sabbath and holiday observance, dress requirements, objection to participation in abortion procedures and payment of union dues.

Many states have similar laws, some of which impose stricter requirements on employers. Most of these laws have relatively short periods of time within which an employee may file a complaint, so a person who believes that he or she has been the victim of religious discrimination in employment should promptly seek legal advice or consult with the local governmental human rights agency.

May an employer force employees to attend religious services?

No, even if the employee is not forced to actually participate in the services.[5]

NOTES

1. 42 U.S.C. § 2000e *et seq.*
2. 42 U.S.C. § 2000e(j).
3. *TWA v. Hardison*, 432 U.S. 63 (1977).
4. *Ansonia Board of Education v. Philbrook*, 479 U.S. 60 (1986).
5. *EEOC v. Townley Manufacturing Co.*, 859 F.2d 610 (9th Cir. 1988).

XV
Prisoners' Rights

No one area of the law of religious liberty will be more directly, immediately, and positively affected by the enactment of the Religious Freedom Restoration Act (RFRA) than prisoner religious practices. Because there was an effort made in the Senate to exclude prison religious liberty claims from the scope of the Act, and that effort was handily rebuffed by the Senate, it is clear that the Act *and* its compelling interest test apply to such claims, which marks a sharp and welcome departure from existing law.

What was the law before the passage of the Religious Freedom Restoration Act?

Even before its unfortunate decision in *Employment Division v. Smith*, the Supreme Court had imposed only a minimal burden on prison officials to justify even substantial burdens on the free exercise rights of prisoners. Specifically, the Court held in *O'Lone v. Estate of Shabazz* that a regulation that interfered with religious liberty would be upheld if it merely had "a logical connection to legitimate governmental interests invoked to justify it"[1] and if "alternative means of exercising the right . . . remain open."[2] This test meant that not quite all claims about religious liberty in prisons failed, as long as prison officials allowed members of a faith some opportunity to exercise their religion, such as owning Bibles or attending chapel services.

What is the standard for evaluating prisoner claims under RFRA?

Under RFRA, prisoner religious liberty claims, like all other claims, are to be evaluated under a compelling interest test. However, the legislative history of the Act makes clear that the courts will "continue the tradition of giving due deference to the experience and expertise of prison and jail administrators in establishing . . . good order, security and discipline, consistent with considerations of cost and limited resources. At the same time . . . inadequately formulated prison regulations . . . grounded on mere speculation, exaggerated fears or post-hoc rationalizations will not suffice."[3]

NOTES

1. 482 U.S. 342, 350 (1987).
2. *Id.* at 351, quoting *Turner v. Safley*, 482 U.S. 78, 90 (1987).
3. S. Res. 103-111, 103d Cong., 1st Sess., at 10.

XVI

The Religious Freedom Restoration Act

What is the Religious Freedom Restoration Act?
The Religious Freedom Restoration Act (RFRA) is a federal
statute designed to restore the traditional protections for religion scrapped by the Supreme Court in *Employment Division
v. Smith*, (1990).[1] RFRA does this by subjecting all laws burdening religious exercise—even facially neutral laws of general
application—to strict scrutiny. Thus, RFRA also overrules parts
of *Goldman v. Weinberger*, (1986)[2] (exempting military regulations from strict scrutiny), and *O'Lone v. Estate of Shabazz*,
(1987)[3] (exempting prison regulations from strict scrutiny by
subjecting military and prison regulations to strict scrutiny).

What triggers RFRA?
Any substantial governmental burden imposed on religious
exercise.

What is meant by religious exercise?
Religious exercise is defined under the Act as "the exercise
of religion under the First Amendment to the Constitution."[4]

**What level of scrutiny does the Act impose on laws bur-
dening religious exercise?**
The Act requires that any law substantially burdening religious exercise be (1) in furtherance of a compelling governmental interest and (2) the least restrictive means of furthering that
compelling governmental interest.[5]

**Do the Act's protections apply to religious organizations as
well as to individuals?**
Yes. RFRA uses the term "person," which is defined in 1
U.S.C. § 1 as including "corporations, companies, associations,
firms, partnerships, societies, and joint stock companies, as
well as individuals."

Does RFRA apply to state and local governments?

Yes. All government action—whether federal, state or local—is subject to RFRA. Moreover, RFRA applies to all laws passed before or after its enactment. Only federal statutes that explicitly exclude application of RFRA are exempt from coverage.[6]

Does RFRA affect the establishment clause?

No. The Act explicitly provides, "Nothing in this Act shall be construed to affect, interpret, or in any way address that portion of the First Amendment prohibiting laws respecting the establishment of religion." In addition, the Act states, "Granting government funding, benefits, or exemptions, to the extent permissible under the establishment clause, shall not constitute a violation of this Act."[7]

Where does one look for guidance in interpreting RFRA?

The legislative history makes clear that courts are expected to look to free exercise of religion cases decided prior to *Smith* for guidance. However, it is also clear that RFRA does not codify the results of any particular case, including those cited in the Act. RFRA expresses no opinion about whether a particular governmental interest is compelling. The Act simply codifies a familiar standard of review to be applied in all cases where religious exercise is burdened. The results in those cases will depend upon the particular facts and circumstances.[8]

NOTES

1. 494 U.S. 872 (1990).
2. 482 U.S. 78 (1987).
3. 475 U.S. 503 (1986).
4. 42 U.S.C. § 2000bb-2(4).
5. 42 U.S.C. § 2000bb-1(b).
6. 42 U.S.C. § 2000bb-3(a) and (b).
7. 42 U.S.C. § 2000bb-4.
8. Religious Freedom Restoration Act of 1993; Report of the Committee on the Judiciary, H. R. Rep. 103-88, 103d Cong., at 6, 7.

XVII
State Constitutions

What impact do state constitutions have on church-state issues?

The Supreme Court has firmly established the right of states to interpret their own constitutions to provide more comprehensive protections than are available under the federal constitution.[1] As one court remarked, a state constitution is "a document whose vitality and force are independent of its federal counterpart."[2] This means that states are free to provide a stricter separation of church and state (as long as the state constitution does not violate federal civil and constitutional rights such as free speech or free exercise)[3] as well as greater protections for the free exercise of religion.

Have some states interpreted their constitutions as requiring a stricter separation of church and state?

Yes. Some states have interpreted their constitutions as forbidding virtually any assistance to religious institutions. For example, providing transportation and textbooks to students attending parochial schools, a practice long permitted under the federal constitution,[4] is prohibited in some states.[5] State courts have been particularly careful to prevent public financial assistance from going to pervasively sectarian institutions such as churches, synagogues, or primary and secondary parochial schools.[6]

This stricter separation of church and state is most likely to be found in states whose constitutions contain language more explicit than the language of the federal establishment clause. Thus, states whose constitutions specify no support for "sectarian" institutions,[7] no support for "private" institutions[8] or no compulsion "to attend or support any ministry, place of worship or denomination"[9] will be more amenable to the separationist view. Conversely, those states whose constitutions either mirror the federal Establishment Clause or prohibit only the preference of a particular religious denomination[10] are less likely to be separationist.[11]

Have states been willing to provide more protections for the free exercise of religion than are available under the federal constitution?

Yes. In the wake of the Supreme Court's decision in *Employment Division v. Smith*,[12] in which use of the traditional strict scrutiny analysis for free exercise claims was sharply curtailed, states have begun interpreting their constitutions to provide greater protection for religious exercise. In *Minnesota v. Hershberger*,[13] for example, the Supreme Court of Minnesota ruled that Old Order Amish could not be forced to display "worldly" orange warning devices on their horse-drawn carriages if more modest silver reflector tape were equally effective in reducing accidents. In ruling for the Amish, the court rejected the *Smith* rule and applied strict scrutiny. Courts in California,[14] Maine,[15] and Massachusetts[16] have also interpreted their state constitutions to provide greater protection for religious exercise.

How important is it to raise state constitutional provisions when litigating a church-state case?

Now more than ever, litigants must invoke state constitutions at the earliest opportunity. The presence of nonseparationists on the United States Supreme Court,[17] as well as the evisceration of free exercise rights in *Smith*, make the use of state constitutions critical to church-state litigation.

NOTES

1. *Robins v. Pruneyard Shopping Center*, 23 Cal. 3d 899, 592 P.2d 341, 153 Cal. Rptr. 854 (1979), *aff'd*, 447 U.S. 74 (1980); *Witters v. Washington Department of Services for the Blind*, 474 U.S. 481 (1986).
2. *Mandel v. Hodges*, 54 Cal. App. 3d 596, 616, 127 Cal. Rptr. 244, 257 (1976).
3. *Garnett v. Renton Area School Dist.*, 987 F.2d 641 (9th Cir. 1993).
4. *Everson v. Board of Education*, 330 U.S. 1 (1947) (transportation); *Board of Education v. Allen*, 392 U.S. 236 (1968) (textbooks).
5. *E.g.*, *California Teachers Association v. Riles*, 29 Cal. 3d 794, 632 P.2d 953, 176 Cal. Rptr. 300 (1981) (textbooks); *Matthews v. Quinton*, 362 P.2d 932 (Alaska 1961), *app. dismissed*, 368 U.S. 517 (1962) (transportation); *Epeldi v. Engelking*, 94 Idaho 390, 488 P.2d 860

(1971), *cert. denied*, 406 U.S. 957 (1972) (transportation); *Bloom v. School Commission*, 376 Mass. 35, 379 N.E.2d 578 (1978) (textbooks); *In Re Advisory Opinion*, 394 Mich. 41, 228 N.W.2d 772 (1975) (textbooks).

6. *Witters v. Washington State Commission for the Blind*, 771 P.2d 1119 (Wash. 1989), *cert. denied*, 493 U.S. 850 (1989).

7. *See, e.g.*, Cal. Const. art. IX, § 8, art. XVI, § 5; Del. Const. art. X, § 3; Mo. Const. art. IX, § 8; Wash. Const. art. IX, § 4.

8. *See, e.g.*, Mass. Const. amend. art. 18, § 2; Mich. Const. art. 8, § 2; Neb. Const. art. VII, § 11.

9. Tenn. Const. art. I, § 3; Va. Const. art. I, § 16.

10. N.J. Const. art. I, para. 4.

11. For an excellent analysis of state counterparts to the Establishment Clause *see* Note, *Beyond the Establishment Clause: Enforcing Separation of Church and State Through State Constitutional Provisions*, 71 Va. L. Rev. 625 (1985).

12. 494 U.S. 872, 110 S. Ct. 1595 (1990).

13. 462 N.W.2d 393 (Minn. 1990).

14. *Donahue v. Fair Employment and Housing Commission*, 2 Cal. Rptr. 2d 32 (Cal. App. 2d 1991).

15. *Rupert v. City of Portland*, 605 A.2d 63 (Me. 1992).

16. *Society of Jesus v. Boston Landmarks Commission*, 409 Mass. 38, 564 N.E.2d 571 (1990).

17. *See Wallace v. Jaffree*, 472 U.S. 38, 90 (1985) (White, J., dissenting); *Wallace v. Jaffree*, 472 U.S. at 91 (Rehnquist, J., dissenting); *Edwards v. Aguillard*, 482 U.S. 578, 610 (1987) (Scalia, J., dissenting); *County of Allegheny v. ACLU*, 492 U.S. 573 (1989) (Kennedy, J., dissenting).

XVIII

Deprogramming

What is deprogramming?

Deprogramming is an effort to alter an individual's religious views following the forcible removal of that person from such a religious group. Deprogrammers assert that some individuals who join religious movements are actually brainwashed into membership by psychological "mind control" techniques combined with physical isolation from persons other than members of that religion.

Is deprogramming lawful?

No. Adults have a right to join any religious or political group with which they come in contact. The Constitution does not draw distinctions between long-established religious groups and newer religions (sometimes disparagingly referred to as "cults").[1] Individuals who remove individuals from their chosen faith may be sued for assault or false imprisonment or even charged with criminal offenses such as kidnapping.

The trend in recent cases is to reject claims by deprogrammers that their actions are legally justified to avoid the individual seized from being "coerced" into losing his or her autonomy. (This is referred to as a "choice of evils" defense.) However, courts are generally unwilling to accept this argument because there are almost always alternative methods to pursue if an individual is deemed to be impaired or in physical danger.[2]

Children (*i.e.*, minors) are generally subject to the control of their parents (*see* chapter 6, above). It may be that parents have the right to prevent their children from adhering to a particular religion. However, it has been suggested that where the wishes of (older) children and parents clash, the rights of children control. This issue has not yet been resolved.[3]

NOTES

1. "The Fathers of the Constitution were not unaware of the varied and extreme views of religious sects, of the violence of disagreement among

them, and of the lack of any one religious creed on which all men would agree. They fashioned a charter of government which envisaged the widest possible toleration of conflicting views. Man's relation to his God was made no concern of the state. He was granted the right to worship as he pleased and to answer to no man for the verity of his religious views. The religious views espoused by respondents might seem incredible, if not preposterous, to most people. But if those doctrines are subject to trial before a jury charged with finding their truth or falsity, then the same can be done with the religious beliefs of any sect. When the triers of fact undertake that task, they enter a forbidden domain." *United States v. Ballard*, 322 U.S. 78, (1944).

2. *See, e.g., Colorado v. Brandyberry and Whelan*, 812 P.2d 674 (Colo. App. 1990); *Eilers v. Coy*, 582 F. Supp. 1093 (D. Minn. 1984).

3. *See generally Wisconsin v. Yoder*, 406 U.S. 205 (1971).

XIX
The Legal System

For many persons, law appears to be magic—an obscure domain that can be fathomed only by the professionals initiated into its mysteries. People who might use the law to their advantage sometimes avoid the effort out of awe for its intricacies. But in fact the main lines of the legal system, and of the law in a particular area, can be explained in terms clear to the layperson. The purpose of this short chapter is to outline some important elements of the system.

What does a lawyer mean by saying that a person has a legal right?

Having a right means that society has given a person permission—through the legal system—to secure some action or to act in some way that she or he desires. For example, a woman might have a right to an abortion, a minority person the right to employment free from discrimination, or a person accused of a crime the right to an attorney.

How does one enforce a legal right?

The concept of *enforcing* a right gives meaning to the concept of the right itself. While the abstract right may be significant because it carries some connotation of morality and justice, enforcing the right yields something concrete—the abortion, the job, the attorney.

A person enforces her or his right by going to some appropriate authority—often, a judge—who has the power to take certain action. The judge can order the people who are refusing to grant the right to start doing so, on pain of a fine or jail if they disobey. The judge can also order the people to pay money to compensate for the loss of the right. Sometimes other authorities, such as federal and state administrative agencies or a labor arbitrator, can take similar remedial action.

The problem with the enforcement process is that it will often be lengthy, time-consuming, expensive, frustrating, and may arouse hostility in others—in short, it may not be worth the effort. On the other hand, in some cases you may not need to go to an enforcement authority in order to implement a right. The concerned persons or officials may not have realized that you have a right and may voluntarily change their actions once you explain your position. Then, too, they may not want to go through the legal process either—it can be as expensive and frustrating for them as it is for you.

Where are legal rights defined?

There are several sources. Rights are defined in the statutes or laws passed by the U.S. Congress and by state and city legislatures. The are also set forth in the written decisions of judges, federal and state. Congress and state and local legislatures have also created institutions called administrative agencies to enforce certain laws, and these agencies interpret the laws in written decisions and rules that further define people's rights.

Are rights always clearly defined and evenly applied to all people?

Not at all, although this is one of the great myths about law. Because so many different sources define people's rights, and because persons of diverse backgrounds and beliefs implement and enforce the law, there is virtually no way to uniformity. Nor do statutes that set forth rights always do so with clarity or specificity. It remains for courts or administrative agencies to interpret and flesh out the details; and in the process of doing so, many of the interpreters differ. Sometimes two courts will give completely different answers to the same question. Whether or not a person has a particular right may depend on which state or city he or she lives in.

The more times a particular issue is decided, the more guidance there is in predicting what other judges or administrative personnel will decide. Similarly, the importance of the court or agency deciding a case or the persuasiveness of its reasoning will help determine the impact of the decision. A judge who states thoughtful reasons will have more influence than one who offers poor reasons.

Law then is not a preordained set of doctrines, applied rigidly and unswervingly in every situation. Rather, law is molded from the arguments and decisions of thousands of persons and institutions. It is very much a human process of trying to convince others—a judge, a jury, an administrator, the lawyer for the other side—that your view of what the law requires is correct.

What is a decision or case?

Lawyers often use these words interchangeably, although technically they do not mean the same thing. A case means the lawsuit started by one person against another, and it can refer to that lawsuit at any time from the moment it is started until the final result is reached. A decision means the written opinion in which the judge declares who wins the lawsuit and why.

What is meant by precedent?

Precedent means past decisions. Lawyers use precedent to influence new decisions. If the facts involved in the prior decision are close to the facts in the present case, a judge will be strongly tempted to follow the former decision. She is not, however, bound to do so and, if persuasive reasons are presented to show that the prior decision was wrong or ill-suited to changed conditions in society, the judge may not follow precedent.

What is the relationship between decisions and statutes?

In our legal system, most legal concepts originally were defined in the decisions of judges. In deciding what legal doctrine to apply to a case, each judge kept building on what other judges had done before him. The body of legal doctrines created in this way is called the common law.

The common law still applies in many situations, but increasingly state legislatures and the Congress pass laws ("statutes") to define the legal concepts that judges or agencies should use in deciding cases. The written decisions of individual judges are still important even where there is a statute because statutes are generally not specific enough to cover every set of facts. Judges have to interpret the meaning of statues, apply them to the facts at hand, and write a decision; that decision will then be considered by other judges when they deal with these statutes in other cases. Thus it is generally not enough to know what a relevant statute defines as illegal; you also have to know how judges have interpreted the statute in specific situations.

What different kinds of courts are there?

The United States is unique for its variety of courts. Broadly speaking, there are two distinct court systems: federal and state. Both are located throughout the country; each is limited to certain kinds of cases, with substantial areas of overlap. Most crimes are prosecuted in state courts, for instance, although there a number of federal crimes prosecuted in federal court. People must always use state courts to get a divorce (except in the District of Columbia and other federal areas), but they must sue in federal court to establish rights under certain federal laws.

In both federal and state court systems one starts out at the trial court level, where the facts are "tried." This means that a judge or jury listens and watches as the lawyers present evidence of the facts that each side seeks to prove. Evidence can take many forms: written documents, the testimony of a witness on the stand, photographs, charts. Once a judge or jury has listened to or observed all the evidence presented by each side, it will choose the version of the facts it believes, apply the applicable legal doctrine to these facts, and decide which side has won. If either side is unhappy with the result, it may be able to take the case to the next, higher-level court and argue that the judge or the jury applied the wrong legal concept to the facts, or that no reasonable jury or judge could have found the facts as they were found in the trial court, and that the result was therefore wrong.

What are plaintiffs and defendants?

The plaintiff is the person who sues—that is, who *complains* that someone has wronged him or her and asks the court to remedy this situation. The defendant is the person sued—or the person who *defends* herself against the charges of the plaintiff. The legal writing in which the plaintiff articulates her or his basic grievance is the *complaint*, and a lawsuit is generally commenced by filing this document with the clerk at the courthouse. The defendant then responds to these charges in a document appropriately named an *answer*. Some states use different names for these documents.

One refers to a particular lawsuit by giving the names of the plaintiff and defendant. If Mary Jones sues Smith Corporation for refusing to hire her because she is a woman, her case will be called *Jones v. Smith Corporation* (*v.* stands for versus, or against).

What is an administrative agency?

Agencies are institutions established by either state or federal legislatures to administer or enforce a particular law or series of laws and are distinct from both courts and legislature. They often regulate a particular industry. For example, the Federal Communications Commission regulates the broadcasting industry (radio and television stations and networks) and the telephone and telegraph industry, in accordance with the legal standards set forth in the Federal Communications Act; and the Interstate Commerce Commission regulates trucking and railroads.

These agencies establish legal principles, referred to as rules, regulations, or guidelines. Rules are interpretations of a statute and are designed to function in the same way as a statute—to define people's rights and obligations on a general scale, but in a more detailed fashion than the statute itself. Agencies also issue specific decisions in cases, like a judge, applying a law or rule to a factual dispute between particular parties.

How does one find court decisions, statutes, and agency rules and decisions?

All these materials are published and can be found in law libraries. In order to find the item desired, one should understand the system lawyers use for referring to, or citing, these materials. Some examples will help clarify the system. A case might be cited as *Watson v. Limbach Company*, 333 F. Supp. 754 (S.D. Ohio 1971); a statute, as 42 U.S.C. § 1983; a regulation, as 29 C.F.R. § 1604.10(b). The unifying factor in all three citations is that the first number denotes the particular volume in a series of books with the same title; the words or the letters that follow represent the name of the book; and the second number represents either the page or the section in the identified volume. In the examples above, the *Watson* case is found in the 333d volume of the series of books called *Federal Supplement* at page 754; the statute is found in volume 42 of the series called the *United States Code* at section 1983; the regulation is in volume 29 of the *Code of Federal Regulations* at section 1604.10(b).

There are similar systems for state court decisions. Once you understand the system, all you need to find out from the librarian where any particular series of books is kept, then look up the proper volume and page or section. It is also important to look for the same page or section in the material sometimes inserted at the back of a book, since many legal materials are periodically updated. A librarian will explain what any abbreviations stand for if you are unfamiliar with that series.

Given this basic information, anyone can locate and read important cases, statutes, and regulations. Throughout this book, such materials have been cited when deemed particularly important, and laypersons are urged to read them. Although lawyers often use overly technical language, the references cited in this book can be comprehended without serious difficulty, and reading the original legal materials will give public employees a deeper understanding of their rights.

What is the role of the lawyer in the legal system?

A lawyer understands the intricacies and technicalities of the legal system, can maneuver within it efficiently and, is able to help people by doing so. Thus the lawyer knows where to find out about the leading legal doctrines in any given area and how to predict the outcome of a case, based on a knowledge of those doctrines. A lawyer can advise you what to do: forget about the case, take it to an administrative agency; sue in court; make a will; and so on. The lawyer then can help you to take the legal actions that you determine are necessary.

How are legal costs determined and how do they affect people's rights?

The cost of using the legal system is predominantly the cost of paying the lawyer for his or her time. Since this has become prohibitive even for middle-class individuals, many people are not able to assert their rights, even though they might ultimately win if they had the money to pay a lawyer for doing the job.

Is legal action the only way to win one's legal rights?

By no means. Negotiation, education, consciousness raising, publicity, demonstrations, organization, and lobbying are all ways to achieve rights, often more effectively than through the standard but costly and time-consuming resort to the courts. In all these areas, it helps to have secure knowledge of the legal underpinnings of your rights. One has a great deal more authority if one is protesting illegal action. The refrain "That's illegal" may move some people in and of itself; or it may convince those with whom you are dealing that you are serious enough to do something about the situation—by starting a lawsuit, for instance.

APPENDIX A
Equal Access Act

A Bill

To protect the free exercise of religion.

SECTION 1. SHORT TITLE.
This Act may be cited as the "Religious Freedom Restoration Act of 1993."

SECTION 2. CONGRESSIONAL FINDINGS AND DECLARATION OF PURPOSES.
(a) FINDINGS.—The Congress finds that—

(1) the framers of the Constitution, recognizing free exercise of religion as an unalienable right, secured its protection in the First Amendment to the Constitution;

(2) laws "neutral" toward religion may burden religious exercise as surely as laws intended to interfere with religious exercise;

(3) governments should not substantially burden religious exercise without compelling justification;

(4) in *Employment Division* v. *Smith*, 494 U.S. 872 (1990) the Supreme Court virtually eliminated the requirement that the government justify burdens on religious exercise imposed by laws neutral towards religion; and

(5) the compelling interest test as set forth in prior Federal court rulings is a workable test for striking sensible balances between religious liberty and competing government interests;

(b) PURPOSES.—The purposes of this Act are—

(1) to restore the compelling interest test as set forth in *Sherbert* v. *Verner*, 374 U.S. 398 (1963) and *Wisconsin* v. *Yoder*, 406 U.S. 205 (1972) and to guarantee its application in all cases where free exercise of religion is substantially burdened; and

(2) to provide a claim or defense to persons whose religious exercise is substantially burdened by government.

**SECTION 3. FREE EXERCISE OF RELIGION PRO-
TECTED.**
(a) IN GENERAL.—Government shall not substantially
burden a person's exercise of religion even if the burden results
from a rule of general applicability, except as provided in sub-
section (b).
(b) EXCEPTION.—Government may burden a person's exercise of religion only ifit demonstrates that application of the
burden to the person—

> (1) is in furtherance of a compelling governmental inter-
> est; and
>
> (2) is the least restrictive means of furthering that com-
> pelling governmental interest.

(c) JUDICIAL RELIEF.—A person whose religious exercise has been burdened in violation of this section may assert
that violation as a claim or defense in a judicial proceeding and
obtain appropriate relief against a government. Standing to
assert a claim or defense under this section shall be governed
by the general rules of standing under Article III of the Constitution.

SECTION 4. ATTORNEYS FEES.
(a) JUDICIAL PROCEEDINGS.—Section 722 of the Revised Statutes of the United States (42 U.S.C. 1988) is amended
by inserting "the Religious Freedom Restoration Act of 1993,"
before "or title VI of the Civil Rights Act of 1964."
(b) ADMINISTRATIVE PROCEEDINGS.—Section 504(b)
(1)(c) of title 5, United States Code, is amended—

> (1) by striking "and" at the end of clause (iii);
>
> (2) by striking the semicolon at the end of clause (iii)
> and inserting "; and"; and
>
> (3) by inserting "(iv) the Religious Freedom Restoration
> Act of 1993" after clause (iii).

SECTION 5. DEFINITIONS.
As used in this Act—
(1) the term "government" includes a branch, department,
agency, instrumentality, and official (or other person acting
under color of law) of the United States, a State, or subdivision
of a State;
(2) the term "State" includes the District of Columbia, the

Commonwealth of Puerto Rico, and each territory and posses-
sion of the United States;

(3) the term "demonstrates" means meets the burdens of
going forward with the evidence and of persuasion; and

(4) the term "exercise of religion" means the exercise of
religion under the First Amendment to the Constitution.

SECTION 6.   APPLICABILITY.

(a) IN GENERAL.—This Act applies to all Federal and
State law, and the implementation of that law, whether statutory or otherwise, and whether adopted before or after the
enactment of this Act.

(b) RULE OF CONSTRUCTION.—Federal statutory law
adopted after the date of the enactment of this Act is subject
to this Act unless such law explicitly excludes such application
by reference to this Act.

(c) RELIGIOUS BELIEF UNAFFECTED.—Nothing in
this Act shall be construed to authorize any government to
burden any religious belief.

SECTION   7.   ESTABLISHMENT   CLAUSE   UNAF-
FECTED.

Nothing in this Act shall be construed to affect, interpret,
or in any way address that portion of the First Amendment
prohibiting laws respecting the establishment of religion (referred to in this section as the "Establishment Clause"). Granting government funding, benefits, or exemptions, to the extent
permissible under the Establishment Clause, shall not constitute a violation of this Act. As used in this section, the term
"granting," used with respect to government funding, benefits,
or exemptions, does not include the denial of government
funding, benefits, or exemptions.

The Equal Access Act and the Public Schools

What triggers the Equal Access Act?

The creation of a "limited open forum." A limited open forum is created whenever a public secondary school provides an opportunity for one or more noncurriculum-related student groups to meet on school premises during noninstructional time. The forum created is said to be "limited" because it is only the school's own students who can take advantage of the open forum. Outsiders are not granted an independent right of access by the Act.

Must a school board create a limited open forum for students?

No. the local school board has exclusive authority to determine whether it will create or maintain a limited open forum. However, if a school has a limited open forum, it may not discriminate against a student group because of the content of its speech.

What is a noncurriculum-related student group?

In *Mergens* the Supreme Court interpreted a noncurriculum-related student group to mean "any student group [or club] that does not *directly* relate to the body of courses offered by the school." According to the Court, a student group directly relates to a school's curriculum *only* (1) if the subject matter of the group is actually taught, or will soon be taught, in a regularly offered course; (2) if the subject matter of the group concerns the body of courses as a whole; or (3) if participation in the group is required for a particular course or results in academic credit.

Schools may not substitute their own definition of noncurriculum-related student group for that of the Court.

Did the Supreme Court give any examples of "noncurriculum related student groups"?

The Court noted that unless a school could show that groups

such as a chess club, stamp collecting club, or community service club fell within the definition of curriculum-related set forth by the Court, they would be considered noncurriculum-related for the purposes of the Act.

In *Mergens*, the Court found at least three groups that were noncurriculum-related for that school: (1) a scuba club, (2) a chess club, and (3) a service club. Each of these clubs was found to be noncurriculum related because it did not meet the Court's criteria set forth in the previous question.

What examples did the Court give of curriculum-related student groups?

The Court noted that "a French club would directly relate to the curriculum if a school taught French in a regularly offered course or planned to teach the subject in the near future. A school's student government would generally relate directly to the curriculum to the extent that it addresses concerns, solicits opinions, and formulates proposals pertaining to the body of courses offered by the school. If participation in a school's band or orchestra were required for the band or orchestra classes, or resulted in academic credit, then those groups would also directly relate to the curriculum."

Who determines which student groups are in fact curriculum related?

Local school authorities, subject to review by the courts. However, the Supreme Court has made clear that a school cannot defeat the intent of the Act by defining curriculum-related in a way that arbitrarily results in only those student clubs approved by the school being allowed to meet.

When can noncurriculum-related student groups meet?

A limited open forum requiring equal access may be established during "noninstructional time," which is defined as time set aside by the school before actual classroom instruction begins or after it ends.

Can noncurriculum-related student groups meet during the school day?

The Equal Access Act is not triggered by student club meetings that occur only during instructional time. The constitutionality of allowing or disallowing student religious clubs to meet during instructional time has not been expressly ruled upon by the Supreme Court.

To what schools does the Act apply?

The Act applies only to public *secondary* schools (as defined by state law) that receive federal financial assistance.

May a school establish regulations for meetings that take place in its limited open forum?

Yes. The Act does not take away a school's authority to establish reasonable time, place, and manner regulations for its limited open forum. For example, a school may establish a reasonable time period on any one school day, a combination of days, or all school days. It may assign the rooms in which student groups can meet. It may enforce order and discipline during the meetings. The key is that time, place, and manner regulations must be uniform and nondiscriminatory.

May schools promote, and teachers participate in, some club meetings and not others in a limited public forum?

Some of the Act's language implies that schools may not sponsor any noncurriculum-related club. Other language suggests that schools can sponsor all noncurriculum clubs except religious ones. Subsequent to the *Mergens* decision, some schools have in fact promoted, or assigned teachers to teach, drama or debate clubs and the like even though the school does not offer formal instruction in these subjects or give credit to those who participate in such clubs. There may be other clubs (such as political clubs) for which school sponsorship is inappropriate. School sponsorship of some noncurriculum-related student clubs does not mean, however, that a limited open forum does not exist or that nonsponsored clubs may meet.

May a school require a minimum number of students to form a noncurriculum-related club?

Not if it "limit[s] the rights of groups of students." Care must be exercised that the school not discriminate against numerically small student groups that wish to establish a club. If the number of clubs begins to tax the available space in a particular school, one teacher might be used to monitor several small student groups meeting in the same large room. The key is to be flexible in accommodating student groups that want to meet.

What does "student-initiated" mean?
It means that students themselves are seeking permission to meet and that they will direct and control the meeting. Teachers and other school employees may not initiate or direct such meetings, nor may outsiders.

May outsiders attend a student meeting?
Yes, if invited by the students and if the school does not have a policy barring all "nonschool persons." However, the nonschool persons "may not direct, conduct, control, or regularly attend activities of student groups."

A school may decide not to permit any nonschool persons to attend any club meetings, or it may limit the number of times during an academic year a nonschool person may be invited to attend.

Obviously, no nonschool person should be permitted to proselytize students who are not voluntarily attending the meeting to which the nonschool person is invited.

May teachers be present during student meetings?
Yes, but there are important limitations. For insurance purposes or because of state law or local school policy, teachers or other school employees are commonly required to be present during student meetings. In order to avoid any appearance of state endorsement of religion, teachers or employees are to be present at student religious meetings only in a "nonparticipatory capacity." The Act also prohibits teachers or other school officials from influencing the form or content of any prayer or other religious activity.

May a teacher or other school employee be required to be present at a student meeting if that person does not share the beliefs of the students?
The Act provides that no school employee may be required to attend a meeting "if the content of the speech at the meeting is contrary to the beliefs" of that employee. If a school establishes a limited open forum, however, it is responsible for

supplying a monitor for every student group meeting if a monitor is required.

Does the assignment of a teacher to a meeting for custodial purposes constitute sponsorship of the meeting?
No.

Does the expenditure of public funds for the incidental cost of providing the space (including utilities) for student-initiated meetings constitute sponsorship?
No.

If a school pays a teacher for monitoring a student religious club, does this constitute sponsorship?
Congressional debate apparently took for granted that payment of a school-required monitor for any club was an "incidental cost of providing the space for student-initiated meetings."

Does the use of school media to announce meetings of non-curriculum-related student groups constitute sponsorship of those meetings?
No. The Supreme Court has interpreted the Act to require schools to allow student groups meeting under the Act to use the school media—including the public address system, school paper, and school bulletin board—to announce their meetings if other noncurriculum-related student groups are allowed to use the school media. Any policy concerning the use of school media must be applied to all noncurriculum-related student groups in a nondiscriminatory manner. Schools, however, may inform students that certain groups are not school sponsored.

Do school authorities retain disciplinary control?
Yes, the Act emphasizes the authority of the school "to maintain order and discipline on school premises, to protect the well-being of students and faculty, and to assure that attendance of students at meetings is voluntary." Furthermore, the school must provide that the meeting "does not materially and substantially interfere with the orderly conduct of educational activities within the school." These two provisions, however, do not appear to authorize a school to prohibit certain student groups from meeting because of administrative inconvenience

or speculative harm. For example, a group cannot be barred at a particular school solely because a similar student group at another school has caused problems.

What about groups that wish to advocate or discuss changes in existing law?

Students who wish to discuss controversial social and legal issues such as abortion, drinking age, the draft, and alternative lifestyles may not be barred on the basis of the content of their speech. The school is not required, however, to permit meetings in which unlawful conduct occurs.

What if some students object to other students meeting?

The right of a lawful, orderly student group to meet does not depend on the approval of other students. All students enjoy the constitutional guarantee of free speech. It is the school's responsibility to maintain discipline in order that all student groups are afforded an equal opportunity to meet peacefully without harassment. The school must not allow a "heckler's veto."

May any groups be excluded?

Yes. Student groups that are unlawful or that materially and substantially interfere with the orderly conduct of educational activities may be excluded. However, a student group cannot be denied equal access simply because its ideas are unpopular. Freedom of speech includes ideas the majority may find repugnant.

Must noncurriculum-related student groups have an open admissions policy?

The Act does not address this issue. There are, however, several federal, as well as state and local, civil rights laws that may be interpreted to prohibit student groups from denying admission on the basis of race, national origin, gender, or handicap.

What may a school do to make it clear that it is not promoting, endorsing, or otherwise sponsoring noncurriculum-related student groups?

A school may issue a disclaimer that plainly states that in

affording such student groups an opportunity to meet, it is merely making its facilities available, nothing more.

What happens if a school violates the Equal Access Act?

The law contemplates a judicial remedy. An aggrieved person may bring suit in a U.S. district court to compel a school to observe the law. Violations of equal access will not result in the loss of federal funds for the school. However, a school district could be liable for damages and the attorney's fees of a student group that successfully challenges a denial by the school board of its right to meet under the Act.

Should a school formulate a written policy for the operation of a limited open forum?

If a school decides to create a limited open forum or if such a forum already exists, it is strongly recommended that a uniform set of regulations be drawn up and made available to administrators, teachers, students, and parents. The importance of having such a document will become clear if the school either denies a student group the opportunity to meet or is forced to withdraw that opportunity. When the rules are known in advance, general acceptance is much easier to obtain.

What about situations not addressed in these guidelines?

Additional questions may be directed to the following organizations, all of whom contributed to this appendix.

American Academy of Religion Department of Religion

American Association of School Administrators

American Federation of Teachers

American Jewish Committee

American Jewish Congress

Americans United Research Foundation

Association for Supervision and Curriculum Development

Baptist Joint Committee on Public Affairs

Christian Legal Society

Department of Education of the U.S. Catholic Conference

First Liberty Institute at George Mason University

General Conference of Seventh-day Adventists

National Association of Secondary School Principals

National Association of Evangelicals

National Conference of Christians and Jews

National Council of Churches of Christ in the U.S.A.

National Council on Religion and Public Education

National Council for the Social Studies

National Education Association

National PTA

National School Boards Association